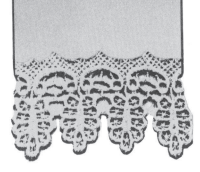

SILK SATINS

The

Sewing Guidebook

For

Twenty Four Hour

Elegance

By **Hazel Boyd-Hooey**

TEX-MAR SEMINARS AND PUBLICATIONS would like to express our thanks to those many individuals and corporations contributing to the development of this seminar and publication: Butterick Fashion Marketing (Vogue/Butterick Patterns); Pfaff Sewing Machine Company; J&P Coats; Laurie Thomas; Hendy Cameron; Pat Parker; Doreen Miller; Larry Solomon; Burda Patterns; N. Jefferson; Marge Brown; Sylvia Sawatzky, Sue Ferguson.

COVER GRAPHICS & DESIGN: JAGER DESIGN

ILLUSTRATIONS: VICKI EASTON, BOB HOOEY,
                             MARGE BROWN, MARC BAUR

TYPESETTING: TICK SET –
                             TERRY AND IRENE CHARLES

PRINTED BY: METROPOLITAN PRESS

PUBLISHED BY: TEX-MAR SEMINARS AND
                             PUBLICATIONS
                             #57 - 10220 Dunoon Drive,
                             Richmond, B.C. V7A 1V6

PRINTED IN CANADA 1987   ISBN -0- 920207-02-2

First Printing January 1986
Second Printing February 1986
Third Printing January 1987

Hazel Boyd Hooey

HAZEL BOYD HOOEY *is a nationally known and respected textile authority, instructor and author.* **COUTURE ACTION KNITS** *and* **SILKS & SATINS** *were her first two successful publications. This is Ms Boyd Hooey's third printing of Silks & Satins, now updated.*

In the development of her seminars and this book, she has again drawn on her vast textile and sewing experiences. The material is presented in an easily understood and quickly applicable format. This publication will help you to sew silks with confidence.

Formerly, Canadian Director for "Knit and Stretch" sewing, she was responsible for development of the Canadian market and recruitment and teacher training across Canada. Further, drawing from her pattern and dress design experience (3 years study in haute couture and pattern drafting under European instruction), seamstress, instructor (Bishop Method and Knit and Stretch) along with a 6 year retail fabric store partnership, she brings a wealth of ideas with time and labour saving techniques.

Presently in addition to her involvement in seminar development for **TEX-MAR SEMINARS**, *she operates an independent sales agency (over 12 years) for several eastern fabric, lace and notion suppliers.*

In spite of her hectic schedule, she does spend some time at the mountain chalet with family and friends. This is where she does most of her design, sewing and wardrobe creation. Proverbs 31:10 through 20 accurately profiles this active lady.

TABLE OF CONTENTS

Wondrous Wearable Silk

For centuries the ultimate luxury of garments made from silk captured the wearers from royalty to the average working class person. On a recent trip to the Isle de' Orleans near Quebec city, we toured the house museum of a doctor from France who was noted for wearing his "silk jacket and trousers". In 1732 that was the order of the day and in the last ten years we've experienced a resurgence of silks again being featured in our wardrobes.

If you have never experienced the joy of wearing silk, you have a treat in store! The touch and elegance which is totally unique to silk has the qualities of being warm in winter and cool in summer. It may come as a surprise to you that silk is a very strong fibre and not as fragile as we have been led to believe.

If you are concerned about the care required; that too will become a simple process as we show you step by step how to successfully wash your silks.

Slinky sumptuous silks are presented in the "Night and Day Intimates" sections. We have taken all the guesswork out of creating beautiful lingerie and loungewear in **Silks & Satins**. With the introduction of nylon into the marketplace, during the past 30 years our lingerie has been mainly made of tricot. In the 1980's the silky satins and crepe de chines, usually cut on the bias, are capturing the highest price tags. We want to show how you can duplicate these romantic items at a fraction of the retail cost.

This guidebook is not intended to replace your basic sewing book but rather, is designed to focus on specialized techniques in working with silk and satin type fabrics.

Luxurious Sewing!

Hazel Boyd Hovey

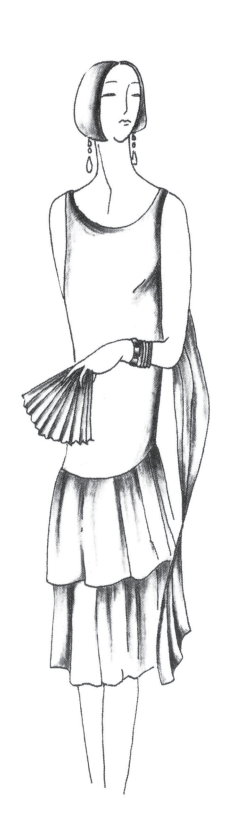

History and Origin of Silk

For over 4000 years this sleek sensuous cloth derived from a member of the caterpillar family has held the position as the "Queen of Textiles". It has been woven into luxurious tapestries, rugs, clothes and accessories for centuries.

There are two types of "silk worms" (as they are called). The commercial or cultivated worm feeds on a diet of Mulberry leaves, producing the finest, silkiest fibres. This specialized diet creates employment for thousands of workers. The Mulberry trees must be cared for, the leaves plucked, chopped and almost spoon fed to the young larvae every few hours. The trees are then pruned and sprayed awaiting the next seasons crop. The Japanese have developed a food substitute by mixing mulberry leaves, soybeans and cornstarch. This could increase production and cut down extensively on labour costs. **It takes 8,000 worms consuming approximately 350 pounds of mulberry leaves to supply enough silk for 10 blouses!**

There are over 500 species of wild silk worms which feast on oak and other leaves, fending for themselves. The tussah worm is considerably larger than the domestic variety, sometimes growing to six inches in length and producing an egg-sized cocoon. Tussah silk has a nubby texture, is stronger and more durable; but does not dye as well. Quite often these silks are sold in the natural shades. China produces some 80% of the world's tussah silk, which is usually an off-white colour. The Assam Valley in India produces a golden coloured tussah which cannot be reeled off the cocoon as with other silks, but instead is spun like cotton or wool.

Unusual eating machines, cultivated silkworms increase their body size 10,000 times in their 25 to 28 day life. They moult four times in this period. After a final moulting they find a place and begin cocooning. They extrude a semi-liquid mixture of protein and a gummy substance called sericin.

This liquid silk is extracted at a rate of about a foot a minute, becoming when exposed to air, the fibre that enshrowds them from the outside in, forming the cocoon.

Unless being saved for egg production, a cocoon is subjected to steam or hot air prior to the worm hatching into a moth, to preserve the silk fibre. The filament length may measure up to a mile! The cocoons are soaked in hot water to soften the sericin, thus enabling thread ends, usually five to eight forming a single strand, to be unravelled and spun together.

Occasionally, two silk worms will nest together forming one cocoon with a double strand. The fibres will give a thick and thin appearance which is known as a Duppioni silk.

In the middle 1800's a severe plague hit the silkworms in an area of France. Louis Pasteur worked for three years to bring this under control. His experimentation and research paved the way in general, for information in the area of infectious diseases, even though many of the looms sat empty.

France and Italy have sophisticated equipment to finish the raw silk and present it ready for garment making. The Italians have prided themselves on their printed silks for centuries. At this time China does not have the machinery to finish fabrics of the quality of these European countries. They are working toward the day when that will not be the case.

Even though silk comprises a mere 0.2 percent of the world's total production of textile fibres, it will continue to be a sought after luxurious cloth for the discriminating woman. Over half of the models in the 1982 Paris Haute-couture shows wore silk. As the New York based designer **Oscar de la Renta** has said: **"Silk does for the body what diamonds do for the hand."**

Did you know? It takes 110 cocoons to make a silk tie and 630 to make a blouse. A heavy silk Kimono would be the work of 3,000 worms, which consumed 135 pounds of mulberry leaves!

Types of Silk Fabric

What's the difference?

SHEER SILKS

Chiffon

A delicate transparent fabric in plain weave. It is very strong, made from highly twisted yarns. This fabric dyes and prints well. It feels like a feather to wear. Lends itself to many layers and lots of fullness for flowing dresses. Sometimes will have satin stripes.

Georgette

A lightweight soft sheer crepe, drapier hand than chiffon. Both silk and polyester georgette tend to grow and move which makes it more difficult to handle in cutting and sewing but the most beautiful sensuous evening dresses are created by leading designers using this fabric.

Organza

A crisp, sheer fabric with plain weave used in puffed sleeve garments and full skirts. Is sometimes printed. Organza also makes an **excellent interfacing** for sheer fabrics. This fabric is also available in stripes.

LIGHTWEIGHT AND OPAQUE SILKS

Broadcloth

Plain woven fabric with somewhat less sheen than most silks. It is ideal for more sporty shirts and blouses and dresses. Occasionally it is striped.

China Silk

Lightweight plain woven silk is made from "silk waste"; shorter silk strands from end of cocoon. A crisper hand is noticeable, as it contains quite a bit of sericin. This silk is best used for linings, etc.

Charmeuse

This fabric has a satin weave with a dull back. The shiny and highly lustrous face gives a sensuous drape. Ideal for lingerie, robes, blouses and evening wear. The soft surface is more susceptible to abrasion.

Crepe de Chine

Plain weave but with yarns tightly twisted to give a crepe or pebbled look. Drapes beautifully. Most popular blouse and dress fabric. Resists wrinkling and washes very well. The majority of printed silk is in this quality.

Crepe Back Satin

High lustrous satin surface and crepe back. Can use both sides for garments – the wearer's preference. This satin is highly used for Bridal wear.

Fuji

Plain close weave. Rather flat surface but with beautiful drape. The two most common weights are 7 lb. and 10 lb. Lovely robes, pyjamas, jumpsuits can be made with this fabric.

Faille

Has a semi-sheen, heavier drape with a cross rib weave. Gives the look of fine horizontal lines. Excellent for dressy evening pants, dresses needing good body and even soft evening jackets.

Tissue Faille is a lighter variety lending itself to blouses and dresses. Due to cost factor Polyester Faille is much more plentiful today than silk.

Habutae

A plain weave similar to china silk. Made from raw silk (not waste) creating a more nubby surface. Use for light garments, lining and shaping.

Pongee

Has a plain rib weave. As this is a very fine lightweight fabric it is hard to differentiate between Habutae, Honan and Pongee. All are ideal for scarves, painting, linings, etc. They have a high sericin content so prewashing is essential.

MEDIUM TO HEAVYWEIGHT SILKS

Boucle

Plain boucled yarn gives this fabric a very nubby texture. Probably the most wrinkle-free silk. It comes in different weights but suits and tailored dresses are most often shown.

Duppioni

Shantung type plain weave. "Du" meaning two cocoons join together to form the slub type yarn. Duppionis quite often come in yarn-dyed stripes in very rich brilliant colours occasionally having a corded effect. The rainbow of plain colours makes co-ordination of this fabric very desirable. They wash extremely well and seem to hold their body better than some other silks. Light suits, dresses, crisp evening blouses are a few suggestions on styles.

Ikat Silk

This is not really a type of silk but a design which is produced by a special dying process. It is usually on a medium weight silk suitable for dresses, shirts and blouses. Patan in India is the area famous for this type of patola weaving. It is a double tie-dye method in which the warp (vertical) and weft (horizontal) yarns are individually knotted and wrapped tight enough with cotton threads that the dye will not penetrate. Designs created from this type of dying are very unusual, giving a rather ethnic look.

IKAT

JACQUARD

Jacquard

Brocade and Damask are both a type of jacquard. Jacquard refers to a woven-in pattern that combines dull and shiney surfaces in a single colour. Subtle dots, flowers and stripes that shimmer are effects which are achieved. Blouses, dresses, nightwear are sumptuous in this drapey fabric. Drycleaning is normally recommended for brocades.

Linen or Heavy Shantung

Plain coarse wild silk producing a thick and thin look. Small little tufts will protrude from the surface which add character to this very natural looking cloth. Shading will occur quite often as the dye doesn't penetrate as evenly in wild silk. A gentle wash will remove enough sericin to eliminate spotting but drycleaning will maintain body in this suiting cloth for the life of the garment.

Noil

A plain weave with small knots in cloth. It is made from short fibres from the cocoon which are spun to form this low lustre silk cloth. It can be used for the more sporty items in your wardrobe including suits, jumpsuits, dresses. It is one of the least expensive silks to purchase, is very durable and crease resistant, but it loses some body when washed. It is often confused with the term "Raw Silk".

Raw Silk

All silk is in this category until the sericin or gummy substance which coats the silk is washed out. The strands are reeled, graded, twisted, washed and wound into skeins. Some silks still retain a high quantity of sericin even after weaving and dying which gives a crisp finish to the fabric.

Silk Knits

The silk in this category is generally in a natural colour stripe or plain. It drapes very well but along with this, stretches considerably after wearing or hanging. A word of caution prior to hemming your garment! The breathability of this type of knit is fantastic. (refer to **COUTURE ACTION KNITS** - the guidebook to sewing with "Knit Know How" by the author.)

Slub Shantung

Plain weave with filling slub or duppioni yarns. Somewhat crisp in texture. Comes in very vibrant almost irridescent colours. Will maintain it's crispness to a greater degree if drycleaned. Washing will soften the fabric.

Taffeta

A plain weave. Usually medium weight. Has a crisp hand and rustles while wearing. Ideal for full evening dresses. The ultimate for a Bridal gown! Moire' taffetta has watery looking embossed swirls which are applied with heat pressure on the surface. Moire' is much more available in acetate and polyester than silk.

MOIRE

Tussah

A type of wild silk. It exceeds mulberry silk in strength and durability but does not dye as well. These worms feed on other than mulberry leaves. It is usually a more yellow toned fabric. In it's natural state, a fabric which has slubs ranging from light to dark brown shading, is produced. A striped effect can be obtained in the weaving (many of this type are hand woven) combining with stripes of colour. Warp (lengthwise) yarns are very fine while the weft (crosswise) yarns are the thick slubby type. There is the chance of the fabric separating while sewing or wearing. Check with the "thumb test" prior to purchasing. The finer types of tussahs generally are more tightly woven. Underlining and lining will relieve pressure on outer fabric.

The foregoing cover the most popular terms and types of fabric available to us in silk.

PRINCIPAL WEAVES

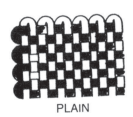

PLAIN

TWILL

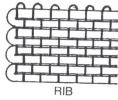
RIB

SATIN

SILK LOOK-ALIKES

Almost all the foregoing silk fabrics have been duplicated with man-made fabrics.

Rayon

(also **VISCOSE**) This was one of the first silk-like fabrics produced in the late 1800's. Rayon dyes well, drapes beautifully and feels like cotton. It's negative features are that it wrinkles very easily and does shrink similarly to silk, so follow the same washing methods. Rayon is a natural (wood/cotton) based fibre and therefore it is very comfortable to wear as it will "breathe".

Polyester

The first commercial production of polyester in the United States was in 1953. It is the most widely used man-made fabric in North America. The original European Trevira was of the heavy doubleknit variety, but today we have some of the most beautiful jacquards, crepe de chines and satins that one can barely tell the difference between pure silk and polyester. The major drawback is the lack of air or water penetration through the fabric. It is very warm in the summer and will hold stains unless a strong soil cleaner is applied in washing. In cold weather, particularly, static is a major problem. Rubbing a little hand lotion on your pantyhose will combat this. Give it a try! In spite of these negatives, it is still one of the greatest easy-care fabrics available today. Very durable and drapes well.

Discharge Printed Polyester

Some of the most beautiful prints coming out of the Orient are of this type. This is a special type of printing where the dye or colour is removed in certain areas leaving them white. The fabric is then direct printed and some or all of the white areas are coloured to provide the pattern desired. This method gives the clearest colours to a print, with the pattern penetrating right through to the wrong side. For those ruffles on the front neck opening of a dress where you do not want a definite right or wrong side, use a discharge print.

WHY THE DIFFERENCE IN PRICE?

You may ask this when comparing a $14.00 per meter Silk Crepe de Chine to a $28.00 per meter one which could be on the same shelf. There are a number of factors which may account for this difference.

1. The $14.00 fabric could have been loosely woven (less threads per square inch of cloth), or the threads twisted to a lesser degree.

2. More expensive silks are quite often dyed more carefully and washed an additional time, thus eliminating some of the shrinkage. The finishing of the fabric can also give a completely different "hand".

3. Choosing an out of season colour will often be cheaper.

4. Colours dyed to a store's specifications to fit in with their co-ordination will increase the price.

Quality is something we learn many times through trial and error. In all probability the more expensive fabric will maintain it's beauty through successive washings, while the cheaper one will look worn. Over time you will come to know by the touch of a fabric the performance it will give.

Silk Blends

Quite often the addition of silk to a fabric will increase the price considerably. Texture is usually the reason for the addition and if this pleases you, make the purchase. If it is added to another natural fibre such as cotton or wool it will still retain its breathability, but adding to a synthetic will take away from this quality. Consider the care factor of the new blend and the percentage of each fibre.

Styles to Compliment

Each type of silk has a special end result that will either enhance or mar it's beauty. Some silks are really lining or scarf weight and if used for regular dresses or blouses will give a rather cheap, lightweight, wrinkled appearance.

> "Like the bride who wanted silk for her bridal attendants and chose China silk in a mandarin collared style, with shirt sleeve and inverted pleat on the back blouse. Before attaching the skirt to the bodice she realized the garment looked like a "dish-rag", very soft but wrinkled and not at all suitable for the style chosen. She took it back to her fabric store for a refund, but the mistake was hers for not discussing fabric and style with the clerk prior to purchasing the very inexpensive but totally inappropriate fabric."

Some silks like Shantung, Duppioni, are too crisp for softer fluid styles where a Crepe de Chine or Jacquard type would create the desired effect.

Refer to Types of Silk Fabric, Page 11 and Silk Shrinkage chart, Page 24 where each type mentioned has suitable garment suggestions.

PATTERN SELECTIONS

K.I.S.S. – Keep it Sophisticated but Simple!

The beauty of silk is enhanced by a relatively simple style. Avail yourself of the ready-to-wear styles in the stores to get cues as to what the leading designers have choosen. Often you will notice the simplicity of the lines and expensive price tags. Most often you will feel less apprehensive spending $75. on fabric when you realize a similar garment in the stores would cost $275. The beauty of sewing your own garments is:

1. You choose the style

2. You choose the colour

3. You can fit the garment perfectly

4. You can preshrink the fabric

5. Most of all your cost is only ¼ to ⅓ the cost of ready to wear

Refer to Pattern Envelope

Fabric suggestions on the pattern envelope generally give suitable selections for the style shown. If in doubt ask your fabric sales clerk for advice.

DRAPE THE FABRIC

Find a full length mirror in the store and drape several fabrics over your shoulder envisioning the style in question. You will soon see if there is too much drape or crispness. All of your fashion designers drape a fabric over a dress form prior to creating a garment so why shouldn't you do the same! (Don't forget to rewind and replace on the shelf!)

MAKE IT COMFORTABLE

Most consultants say that a looser fit will mean less wrinkling. For wearing comfort, commercial patterns usually allow 2 inches of ease or excess fabric over your measurements for dresses, slacks, skirts, etc., and 4 inches for jackets and coats. When you flat measure your pattern prior to cutting out ensure that you have the above suggested minimums.

Dropped shoulder styles where tight armholes are eliminated give a feeling of "airiness" and decrease problems of perspiration. Fullness, gathers, cowl neck styles are ideal for the soft drapey silks. The firmer heavier, crisp ones are best used in more tailored styles.

SEPARATES EXTEND YOUR WARDROBE

When possible make a skirt and blouse rather than a dress. Adding a pair of slacks to a skirted suit will give increased versatility.

Caution!! when choosing two or three different colours to be sewn into same garment. If you wish to wash the finished product, colours may bleed into each other. Drycleaning would eliminate this risk.

DUPLICATING A PREVIOUS GARMENT

Using a style already tried will take much of the guesswork out and give confidence to create a beautiful finished product on the first try. Many times changing the fabric gives an entirely different look, not to mention the savings on the purchase of a pattern.

STYLES FOR THE LARGER FIGURE

Most pattern companies have a group of specially styled patterns for the larger sizes. Silks are very slenderizing, yet perfect for a sophisticated look; bearing in mind our K.I.S.S. rule.

Fabric Preparation

If well cared for, silk garments can become heirlooms. European women have grown up with a reverence for silk fabric and an intimate knowledge of it's care. Our "wash and wear" culture is misinformed on how to care for silk and thus harbours an unnecessary fear of this cloth.

Washing will remove any sericin residue still in the cloth, giving the fabric a softness which in some cases may not be desirable. **Suiting weights** will maintain their crispness and body if they are **drycleaned**. I have found however, that to prewash even these silks, will eliminate future water spotting and possible shrinkage. One washing does not seem to harm the look.

One of the advantages of sewing your own garment lies in the fact that you **can pre-wash** your fabric. Bear in mind that women have been washing silk for centuries without the aid of drycleaners so why can't you? Even though all silks can be drycleaned, most can be washed.

> ***Pre-test:*** Take a small piece of fabric and preshrink to see whether you like the texture, colour change if any and the amount of shrinkage which takes place.

PREWASHING SILK

Small pieces can be washed in your sink, larger ones in the bathtub.

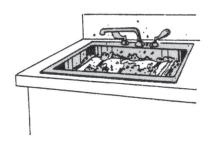

1. Use lukewarm water (cold will not remove oils). Put a small amount of liquid dish detergent (Ivory is very gentle) or protein shampoo in water (some have conditioners, so read label). Remember, silk is like your hair – so treat it with care!

2. Place fabric in water and swish around for a few minutes. Squeeze **(do not twist or wring)** fabric on the sides of sink.

3. Rinse with cool water several times. It is important to remove all soap. To ensure this you can add one-quarter cup white vinegar to final rinse.

4. Strong colours will appear to bleed. This excess dye normally ceases after a couple of washings. To help set the dye you may add a few shakes of salt to the final cold rinse. Press fabric on sides of sink to remove most of the water.

5. Roll fabric in towel to absorb moisture. Take immediately to iron and press on wrong side slowly moving from side to side with warm dry iron. If ironing a strong coloured fabric, you may want to put a cloth or light towel on ironing board to absorb any excess colour which may come out while pressing. If you cannot iron immediately, put garment in a plastic bag and refrigerate (not for more than a day as mildew will set in). Some silks do not retain wrinkles if they are drip dried and then pressed with steam. Shiny spots caused by metal in dye can be eliminated by use of a see-through press cloth or by pressing on wrong side of garment. You can also dampen with mist sprayer. No fear of water spotting as the gum and sericin which cause this have been washed out.

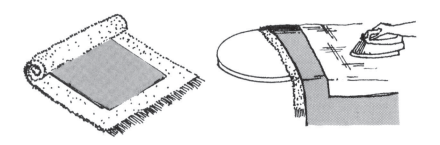

Silk Shrinkage Chart

TYPE	WEAVE	QUALITIES	CARE	SHRINKAGE	APPLICATIONS
Habutae	plain close-weave fine thread	lightweight, soft–good silk for scarves	hand wash separately in cold water–drip dry warm to hot iron (steam)	5%	linings, scarves loose blouses fabric painting
Taffeta	plain close-weave	medium weight, stiff finish	dry-cleaning recommended	5%	evening wear blouses occasion dresses
Twill	twill close weave fine thread	strong, light, excellent dye quality	"	1%	art (hanging) linings, scarves lingerie, blouses
Raw Silk Noil	plain weave count average	heavier weight, durable, crease resistant, nubby	can be dry cleaned to retain stiffer hand, very washable	6¼%	all types clothing blouses, robes jumpsuits, trousers
Fuji 2 weights	plain close weave	medium weight, durable, lovely body and drape	"	8%	dresses, jumpsuits, blouses, skirts, shorts, pyjamas
Mix 50%Noil 50%Fuji	plain weave count average	medium weight, soft finish with good drape/body	"	9%	blouses, skirts, robes, knickers, suits, pants
Boucle 2 weights	plain boucled yarn	durable, crease-resistant, full weight drape	dry-clean recommended (wash like a knit) lay flat to dry	6%	jackets, pullovers, lined skirts, loose pants
Crepe de chine	plain with yarns very twisted	light/medium, soft but strong, excellent drape	hand wash separately (cool water) rinse well steam iron	10%	blouses, lingerie, evening wear, dresses, jumpsuits
Jacquard	plain Jacquard over shot	sometimes crepey sometimes more flat finished	"	5 - 10%	camisoles, robes, pyjamas, skirts, kimonos
Slub Shantung	plain with filling slub yarns	good weight & body for suits low lustre	" can be dry-cleaned to retain stiff hand	2 %	cullotes, jackets, dresses, lined suits, painting
Heavy Shantung	plain coarse threaded	heavy; stiff before dry-cleaning or steaming	dry-clean: will pill if washed (softened) too much	3%	suiting (lined), coats interior design uses pants
Satin & Charmeuse	welt over-slides 4 warps	shiny & highly lustruous face sensuous drape	hand-wash separately rinse out all soap steam iron	5%	occasion dresses, lingerie, camisoles, robes, ensembles

> ***Suggestion:*** If you have a rather large quantity of fabric to wash. I have used my new washer on a delicate cycle for just about every type of silk, Crepe de chines, Jaquards, Silk linens, etc. With Noil, I found some streaking took place. Using your dryer on a cool setting for **partial drying** is possible but this may soften your crisper fabrics too much.

MEASURE your preshrunk piece of fabric. Make notes in a fabric swatch book of the shrinkage. **Always purchase 5% more fabric** to allow for shrinkage. This is a minimum amount, it may be more for some fabrics.

DRYCLEANERS ARE NOT INFALLIBLE!

A friend's Silk Shantung dress shrunk one whole size when sent to the cleaners for pressing, following construction. They used steam  and because the fabric had not been preshrunk, the inevitable happened. You can steam your fabric by laying it on a bed holding iron closely over (2 inches approximately) to pre- shrink. You may use an old sheet to protect bed. Or have the drycleaners preshrink your fabric.

Keep Your Silks Clean

Do not allow perspiration build up on silks. **This will destroy fabric!** Silks get lovelier with each successive washing. Moths will attack dirty silk! Use dress shields if you have perspiration problems.

DO NOT DRY SILKS NEAR A WINDOW OR SUNLIGHT

SPOT REMOVAL

1. **TEST** any removal products on a small swatch or corner to test dye and finish.

2. When in doubt – take it to the cleaners as quickly as possible.

3. **EASY WASH** – This fine spot remover product contains no bleach or caustic ingredients. Excellent for most silks but test first.

4. Do not store spotted garments. They could be permanently damaged.

5. **NEVER** touch blood or heavy perspiration stains on silks. They require special products only available to dry cleaners.

6. Many beverage spills coffee, tea, red wine, juices, soft drinks can be treated with Easy Wash; Neutral Soap; tepid water; white vinegar or lemon juice and respond well if handled quickly.

7. Use a spray bottle, place a towel underneath and spray around spot and then directly on spot.

8. Wash and rinse entire garment in neutral soap solution.

9. **BLEACH: NEVER USE chlorine bleach.** Sample test with a dry oxygen bleach like Clorox II. Bleaches tend to yellow silk fibres.

 **Silks will fade** very easily if they are subjected to light even briefly. One friend hung her folded fabric over a dining room chair for a few days until she was ready to cut out. The beautiful border print was ruined by faded edges on every fold of the fabric.

Notions and Accessories

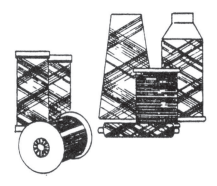

THREAD

There are some seamstresses that feel silk or cotton thread, being natural fibres are the only suitable types for silk sewing. I have used all types on various silks and experienced no problems.

Silk Thread

 Is very expensive but does blend well with silk fabrics. It is very strong also, but is a heavier denier than other threads. I save my silk thread for topstitching, using a slightly larger needle size. It has a lovely sheen which will enhance your garment. The only drawback is the limited colour selection. Somehow it does reflect the colour sewn even if the match isn't perfect. Do not leave in sunlight as it will fade.

Cotton Thread

Pure cotton thread is very difficult to find in a finer weight than 50 denier. It has no give or stretch and therefore should never be used on bias cut garments or bindings. On lighter weight silks it can appear ridgy on the seamline. One recommendation for using cotton thread is that it being weaker than the fabric, your seam would rip prior to the garment tearing if put under stress.

Polyester / Cotton Wrapped

J & P Coats put this product out in their Koban quality. The centre part of the core is polyester which is covered with cotton. This quality is in a 120 denier weight, slightly finer than many of the European polyesters available. This combination is excellent for silk in that the cotton being next to the silk fibre diminishes the possibility of the polyester yarn cutting the fabric because of it's strength.

Polyester Spun (Long Fibre)

This thread has stretch and give making your seam more elastic. It has many other features; shrink and tear resistant, soft-fine, washfast, fade resistant. There are many European qualities on the market: Ackermann; Amann; Gutterman; Metrosene; Molynycke. The thread denier varies to some degree for each company anywhere from 100D to 140D, for regular homesewing. The finer thread is by far the nicest for silk sewing and these polyester threads are generally promoted for all types of fabric, including silk.

Serger Threads

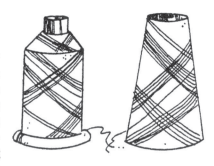

With the introduction of the serger to the world of homesewing, thread companies have been clamouring to put out the larger cones for consumer use. An extremely fine yarn is required, as the layering of three to four threads on top of one another can create a very bulky appearance. Purchasing a large cone **does not necessarily mean you will get a fine thread**. As a matter of fact some of the larger cones are the poorest quality threads with "whiskers" all over.

One of the finest I have located is J & P Coats "Brilliant" thread. It is a Poly/Cotton wrapped thread of the finest 225 denier, mercerized (preshrunk), with the fuzzies burned off, yet retaining the high sheen finish. It is amazing how three threads can be twisted so fine without a flaw! This is the type of thread manufacturers use in the construction of their garments.

Currently it is available only through sewing machine outlets, however they are working on availability to regular fabric stores. Watch for other brands to come on the market with this same quality.

> ***Caution!*** Watch that you are actually getting a finer thread on the larger spools as some companies are using their regular thread for this put-up.

Rayon Thread

This is a very silky looking thread which is lovely for rolled edges on the serger, applique and topstitching. It gives a very decorative look. This is only available in the very large spools at present and is hopefully coming out in smaller put-ups for the homesewer.

What colour should I choose for Serging?

> Purchase neutral colours, ivory, beige, black, grey, etc., as in most cases serged seams are on the inside. The most important thread to colour match is the needle thread, as it will sometimes show on the right side.

Buttonhole Thread Test

Take several brands of sewing thread and make a sample buttonhole with each kind. Looking at the finished product will most readily demonstrate the differences in thread quality.

Topstitching

SILK THREAD – (heavier quality) use a size 80/12 machine needle. Lengthen stitch and sew slowly. Use a seam guide if you need a line to follow.

BUTTONHOLE TWIST – polyester thread is very heavy. If you wish that look use a size 90/14 to 100/16 needle. Be careful that this does not puncture large holes in fabric. **TEST** first!

Can't find the right colour for topstitching? – Combine two thicknesses of your regular thread and thread onto machine as one, lengthening your stitch.

PINS AND NEEDLES

The variety and choice of pins and needles is steadily increasing for homesewers.

Pins

SHARP (not ballpoint) pins are a must for use on silk fabric; Long, Extra Fine, Extra Long-extra fine, Long Glass Headed. Wedding Dress and Lace Pins are designed specifically for fine and light coloured fabrics. These stainless steel pins will not mark or rust delicate silks.

LACE PINS – are made of Brass and are only suitable for lace work. They are not recommended for dressmaking as they tend to bend easily.

Needles

REGULAR SHARP MACHINE NEEDLES, not ballpoint are required, using fine 65/70 - 9/10, for the lightweight silks and graduating up as you work on heavier fabrics. Most blousing and lingerie fabrics would be in the fine category up to Shantungs and suiting weights which require Medium 80/90 - 12/14. (European and American sizes) **NEVER sew over pins!** However, should this happen, **THROW OUT NEEDLE.** Change needle at beginning of each major project. Occasionally with crisp silk, the sericin from the fabric will accumulate on the tip of the needle and create a crunchy sound. Try sewing on some plain cotton muslin to clean the needle.

HAND SEWING NEEDLES – should be varied according to weight of fabric. The finest needle should be used on your lightweight lingerie and soft fabrics. A mixed package of needles gives a variety from 3 to 9 (10 is the finest size).

BUTTONS

Check the ready-to-wear fashions for ideas on buttons for silks. **Simple button styling adds class to a garment.** Covered buttons may not always be the answer as they can project that "loving-hands-at-home" look. A single covered button at the back of the neck is always acceptable. The buttons-to-cover with the shank attached to the top of the button will eliminate the top of the button falling off while buttoning the garment. Silk blouses quite often have the greyish mother-of-pearl flat buttons. They seem to pick up the colour of the garment. See Special treatments chapter, Page 123 for fabric buttons.

PIPING

Many decorative pipings are available to enhance seams; satin, polyester and poly/cotton. Achieve that couture look by making your own piping from self fabric applying it on edge seams, dropped shoulder seams, etc. Be sure to preshrink the string which

PIPING SEWN

you put in the piping trim. See Lingerie Chapter, Page 86 for bias trims.

SCISSORS AND SHEARS

Silk tends to dull scissors. Sharpen your shears as often as needed. A good pair of scissors will last for years and is an excellent investment.

Pinking shears are ideal for silks when finishing is not desired.

ROTARY CUTTER
Watch your fingers – It's very sharp!

These cutting tools are extremely quick and accurate to use. Use weights to hold the pattern onto fabric. These can be purchased or use what you have, glass furniture castors, ashtrays, etc. A special cutting mat **must be used** to protect blade and table surface. These come in various sizes and will last for years. The cutters are available with or without a seam quide. The guide can be removed if needed. Several thicknesses can be cut at one time if you are cutting more than one garment. This is an excellent method for silk as you do not lift the fabric while cutting, giving a very straight edge.

ROTARY CUTTER

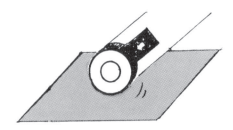

MARKING EQUIPMENT

The main consideration is the delicacy of silk, and the possibility of leaving permanent marks on the fabric.

Dressmaker's pencils come in different colours and the new water soluble or evaporating marking pens are excellent. Don't forget that the garment must be sewn within 24 hours or the marks disapear. On the finer fabrics, tracing wheels may leave permanent marks – check first! See Layout and Cutting, page 45.

SHEER TRICOT BIAS SEAMS FINISH

Comes in black, white and beige in a sheer bias about 5⅜" wide. When applying to finish a seam, stretch slightly and it will roll over edge making it very easy to stitch. Use a multiple zig-zag if available. Very nice for an unlined jacket.

FIX IT VELOURS OR VELCRO

Use this for fastening shoulder pads in place. They can then be removed for cleaning and pressing. When you would like to eliminate buttonholes on shoulders and hidden areas, use the little circular button type closures. See Shoulder Pads, page 34.

FRAY CHECK

This clear plastic liquid can be used to keep buttonholes, corners, serger seam ends and pockets, etc. from fraying out. The liquid will dry darker so apply very cautiously. Be careful not to put it on the garment as it tends to absorb further than you desire. Test first to help you decide if it is wise to use on your silk. Use a toothpick to control application. It will handle laundering and dry cleaning.

Shoulder Pads

Use shoulder pads to fill out and give support to areas where definition is required. These may be purchased or self-made in a variety of shapes and sizes. We've included the main ones used in women's wear.

1. ¼″ (6mm); ½″ (1.3cm) used for set-in sleeves in dresses, blouses, jackets. These are normally covered in an acetate lining with finished or unfinish  ed edges. Can be covered with matching fabric resulting in an attractive finish to the unlined garment. This also eliminates obvious show through to the right side of garment. Cut your fabric on the bias for ease in shaping over the pad allowing 1″ (2.5cm) seams. On underside, tack lining to pad by folding back, working across pad with slanted basting stitches. Catch tiny stitches on lining side. Place top piece on and serge stitch edges together. Nylon tricot in a matching colour also works well.

2. 1″ (2.5cm) used for set-in sleeves in lined coats and jackets. This pad extends below the shoulder providing a smooth foundation in the upper chest area, a common problem problem in this area for most women.

3. ¼″ (6mm); ½″ (1.3 cm); 1″ (2.5cm) used for raglan, dolman or kimono sleeves and dropped shoulders. Use ¼″ for blouses,  sweaters and for lightweight dresses and ½″ for dresses and soft jackets. Use 1″ (2.5cm) for lined coats and jackets. Often the sleeve portion of the pad is broader than shown which gives an extended shoulder look.

Easy Application

Try using Velcro or Fix Velour for applying shoulder pads to garment. The pads can then be easily removed for washing and dry-cleaning, not to mention the ease in pressing the garment. The smaller button type may be used. Velcro glue may be carefully used to apply velcro to pads and garment on seam allowance. **It is best to place fuzzy side on garment.**

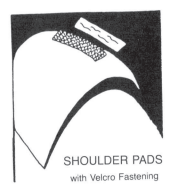

SHOULDER PADS
with Velcro Fastening

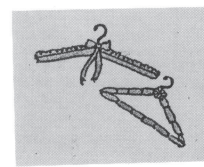

Purchase or make some of those beautiful **satin padded hangars.** The shoulder lines of your garment will maintain their shape and the special care will enhance your silk for years to come.

Use a small piece of "magic tape" to secure the ends of thread on spools. Keeps your sewing drawer tidy and organized.

Interfacing for Silks and Satins

Choosing the correct interfacing for your silk garment is one of the more important steps to consider. A very lightweight interfacing will be required to maintain the beauty of the look with the softer silks. Sometimes using a piece of self fabric is sufficient to give just enough body to a garment. Suiting silks should be treated much like other fabrics. Select interfacing weight in conjunction with fabric weight. A balance must be correct for the desired outcome. Place fabric and interfacing together and **TEST** for durability and show-through to the right side. Today, a vast assortment of colours are available; nude, ivory, white, black, charcoal and grey. On lightweight fabrics, pure white has a tendency to show through, whereas nude or ivory do not detract from the colour. Keep in mind the intent when the selection is made.

WOVEN INTERFACING

This type comes in fusible or non-fusible. One of the most popular lightweight fusible interfacings used with silks is Presto Sheer, white, ivory or black. Refer to the following chart listing most suitable interfacings available. Woven types can be cut on the bias, if you wish to shape an area, such as the collar.

NON-WOVEN INTERFACING

This type also comes in fusible or non-fusible. The majority of non-woven fusibles have a crosswise stretch but retain lengthwise stability which prevents stretching in vertical buttonholes, waistbands or pockets, etc. If you choose a non-woven with a crosswise stretch you will need to run the stretch up and down when using **horizontal buttonholes** to prevent bubbling.

Poly-O a very lightweight fusible, is excellent for your fine silks. The knitted fusibles are very nice in the fabric types with some body. I have found them to be somewhat heavy for the lighter types. The interfacing chart lists most of the compatible types.

PRE-SHRINK WOVEN OR KNITTED FUSIBLES

Hand immerse interfacing piece in **HOT** water. This does not harm its fusibility as resin is activated only at higher boiling temperature (300 deg.F). Soak for approximately 20 minutes. Do not rub the fabric as this tends to remove fusible surface finish. Roll in towel to remove all excess moisture and hang over shower rod to dry. In testing the very lightweight woven interfacing which is excellent for silk, I found that there was no shrinkage at all. Improvement has obviously been made over the years, so experiment and measure for yourself and you may decide that pre-washing is not necessary. I always pre-shrink a good sized piece so that it is ready for whenever I may need it.

NON-WOVEN FUSIBLES

These do not generally shrink but, prior to cutting you may check by placing a pressing cloth on ironing board, then interfacing with fusible side down. Hold steam iron 2 inches above. You may see the interfacing pull in slightly. Continue with steaming until this action stops.

INTERFACING AREAS

Pattern pieces mixed up? Place a piece of "magic tape" on wrong side of fabric. You can label each piece as this tape has a dull finish which retains writing.

Interfacing for Silks 'n Satins

	FABRIC NAME	TYPE	WEIGHT	FIBRE CONTENT	COLORS	USE
FUSIBLES						
⊗	Easy Knit	knit	light	100% nylon	W, Bl, B, G	- soft drapable tricot with crosswise stretch & lengthwise stability
**	Fuse A Knit	"	"	"	W, Bl, I	Molds well – Good for silks
••	Knit Shape	"	"	"	Bl, B, C	
■	Poly "O"	non-woven fusible	sheer	100% Polyester	W, B, C	- no show through – Good for silks / - crosswise stretch / - stability for sheer - ltwt fabrics
••	Sheer Shape	"	"	"	W, B	blouses, dresses, for minimal shaping
**	Stylease	"	sheer & lt	"	W, I, C	"
••	Shape Well	woven	med wt	100% cotton	W	-woven med wt, cut on bias for knits, adheres well
**	Stylemaker 601	Woven	Lightweight	60% Poly/40% Rayon	I, C	No flexibility. Good for silks, lightweight types
**	Stylemaker 602	"	Med		I, C	Good for lightweight suits
⊗	Shape Flex	"	ltwt	100% cotton	W, Bl	Woven ltwt, adheres well
■	All-Purpose					
**	Every Purpose	"	ltwt	"	W, Bl, I	Excellent for silks
**	Presto	"	ltwt	"	"	Excellent for silks
**	Presto Sheer	"	sheer	"	"	Excellent for silks & sheers
■	Jiffy Flex	Non-woven	1. Super ltwt	100% Polyester	W	Crosswise stretch
		"	2. Super - ltwt	80% Poly/20% nylon	W, C	soft flexible shaping
⊗	Easyshaper	"	3. Suitwt		W, C	Jacket wt silks, collar shaping
		"	ltwt	70% nylon/20% poly/10% rayon	W, C	Same as Jiffy Flex #2
**	Lastick	"	suitwt	100% Poly	W, C	Same as Jiffy Flex #3
		"	Med wt		W	Same as Jiffy Flex #2

Code	Name	Type	Weight	Fiber Content	Colors	Uses
★★	Stylemaker 603	woven brushed	med	56% rayon, 44% cotton	W, B	- brushed surface, soft shaping, non-stretchy, suits
●●	Sof-Shape	Non-woven	Lt to Med	100% nylon	W, I, C	for soft natural shaping brushed surface crosswise for bias stretch
■	Shape-up	Non-woven	Medium	100% spunlaced Poly	W	Molds well for lightwt suits
●●	Feather Shape	"	"	60% viscose 40% nylon computer dot	W	
⊗	Suit Shape	Woven Weft Insertion	Medium	84% Nylon, 16% rayon	G, W	brushed surface suit wt and heavier silks – tailored garments
★★	Stylemaker 603	"	"	56% Rayon, 44% cotton	B	"
★★	Acro Fusible non-fusible	woven haircanvas	med haircanvas	70% Rayon, 21% Polyester 9% Hair	B	Heavier coats
■	Suitmaker	fusible woven	medium haircanvas	48% Cotton, 39% Rayon, 13% Goat's Hair	B	Heavier suits coats

WOVEN NON-FUSIBLE

Code	Name	Type	Weight	Fiber Content	Colors	Uses
★★	Sew Sure	Woven	Soft, med firm	50% Poly, 50% Rayon	W, Bl	Med. wt silk garments
■	Durable press	50/50 woven	Med	50% Poly, 50% Rayon	W, B	"
⊗	Veriform		medium	—	W, Bl	Suits, jackets
■	Shaping Aid	100% Rayon	lt wt	100% Rayon	W	Soft pliable. ltwt garments
	Organza	Silk or Poly	Sheer Crisp	Silk or Poly	—	Sheer blouses, collars, cuffs, etc.
	Self-fabric	Silk	Ltwt.	Silk	—	China Silk, Pongee, Poshan
	China Silk	"	"		I	Dresses, blouses

Colors:
W - white
Bl - black
I - ivory
C - charcoal
G - grey

PRE-SHRINK FUSIBLE INTERFACINGS SEE PAGE 37.

Fabric Company Codes:
⊗ Stacy Fabrics Corp.
■ Staple Sewing Aids
★★ J. N. Harper
●● Pellon Corp.

Necklines, tabs, waistbands, collars, cuffs and facings should all be interfaced. Interfacing helps retain detailing and stability while preventing excess stretching. Patterns sometimes do not suggest interfacing in areas where it would be beneficial. For example; a dress with a bias back diagonal seam on the skirt section needs to be stabilized with interfacing on the facing side of the opening. This is often not mentioned in the pattern. **FUSING ON THE FACING SIDE** is generally suggested. This eliminates any possibility of showing through. It is not normally necessary to interface hemlines as this can distract from the softness desired with many fabrics. Obvious drapey styled areas would also be excluded. One exception however, is your jacket hem. Mark hemline with basting stitches, or press up a hem width. Next, machine or hand finish raw edge. Cut a bias piece of fusible interfacing the same length as hem (piecing as necessary). Iron interfacing to wrong side of hem using standard application techniques. Hem garment using a blind catch stitch (see page 75), easing in fullness where necessary and press.

HERE'S HOW TO FUSE

1. Place pattern piece carefully on interfacing so the grainline arrow on pattern follows the lengthwise grain direction of interfacing. Cut.

2. Trim away ½ inch (1.3cm) off seam allowances. The remaining ⅛ inch (0.3cm) is stitched into seam in the event of future release of your interfacing at some point. Trim ¼ inch (0.6cm) off corners to reduce bulk.

COLLAR STAND   CUFF

COLLAR

TRIM ½ INCH (1.3CM) OFF SEAM ALLOWANCES

A handy grab all storage unit may be made from a mug rack hung on your wall. Use for notions and tools needed often.

3. Place coated side of interfacing on wrong side of fashion **fabric facing.** Cover with damp press cloth and apply steam and pressure for **ten seconds** (count slowly) with iron set on "wool". Do not slide iron. Turn fabric over and using a press cloth repeat for an additional ten seconds.

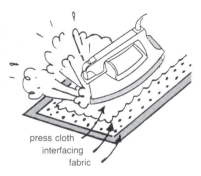

press cloth
interfacing
fabric

What's a Momme (m/m)?

What is this term? It is a Japanese unit of weight equal to 3.75 grams, used to determine the weight of silk fabrics. The weight of fabric increases with the number of threads per square inch. Crepe de Chines are most often referred to as being a 14mm or 16mm as an example. The general scope is 12mm to 18mm. Printed crepe de chines are usually 14mm. After handling silks for awhile you will become more familiar with the feeling of the different weights.

Fast Fitting Tips

As mentioned in our Styles to Compliment section, making your silk garment comfortable with adequate ease will alleviate some of your fitting problems.

SILKS SHOULD NEVER FIT TIGHTLY! The loosely woven types could tear at the seams. Extra fabric or wear ease at the armholes, seat of the pants or hipline should be minimum 5 to 6 cm (2″ to 2⅜″) but the design ease could be up to 10 to 15 cm (4″ to 6″). Looser garments do not reveal the body's imperfections.

TRY ON PATTERN

Flat measure your pattern according to the above suggestions for ease and pin pattern tissue together, seam to seam and slip on. Ask a friend to assist you in making any alterations. Tucks and adjustments are made much easier on paper prior to pattern cutting. Follow any of your pattern firms' sewing books on the basic fitting techniques. Most newer patterns have their adjustment instructions printed for you on the patterns themselves.

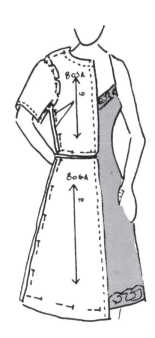

If you have a lower rounded neck or V neck a small tuck can be placed in the tissue or with the following technique.

EASING V-NECK STYLES

Because a V-neck is in fact on the bias, it is highly possible the neck will gape. This method will eliminate that possibility and give a perfect fit each time. When self trims, instead of facings, are used to finish a neck edge it would be more important to consider this method.

A V-neck can be "held in" by means of a stabilizer. This is in the form of pre-shrunk seam binding.

1. Measure from shoulder point to point of V. Take tiny tuck as shown at middle point of V-neck, approximately ¾" (2cm). Fit pattern on body for exact amount needed.

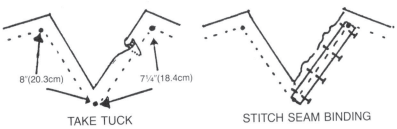

8"(20.3cm)   7¼"(18.4cm)

TAKE TUCK   STITCH SEAM BINDING

2. Cut pieces of seam binding, measurement with tuck folded. Place pieces for both sides. Place on wrong side keying up shoulder and V-point, over seamline.

3. From right side, distribute fullness evenly along tape and pin in place.

4. Hand baste or machine baste binding to neck.

5. Steam smooth, by placing over ham, or on a press mitt which can be slipped over the end of a sleeve board.

6. Finish neck with desired method, facing or bias.

Full Length Mirror is a must for the serious seamstress. Check at each stage of garment construction for detail development as well as a total head-to-toe general appearance.

Layout and Cutting

Because of the delicacy of silk there may be some apprehension about cutting into that luscious piece of cloth. The main problem encountered with the satin types is slippage of the fabric while laying out and cutting. Here are some tips which may help cut down on your frustration.

CUTTING BOARD

These are made of cardboard and are marked with inches in each direction to provide for accurate placement of fabric on true grain

in all directions. Fabric will not slide on this surface. Long pins can be stuck into the board to hold your pattern pieces firmly in place. The board may be permanently secured to a tabletop if you have a sewing room or be folded for easy storage. They are very inexpensive and can extend your cutting area. (6ft × 3ft/182cm × 91.5 cm)

PADDED CUTTING BOARD

This can easily be made for a permanent sewing accessory. Canvas blocking cloths on which 1 inch (2.5cm) lines are drawn are available in knitting and stitchery stores. Prepare a piece of plywood 48"(122 cm) by 54" (137 cm) using old flannelette sheets for a thickness of about ½" (1.27cm) padding. Cover tightly with canvas and staple sides to the wood. Slippery fabrics remain stationary for cutting, while pins can be pushed into it's surface. Additionally, it gives a large area for pressing.

ROTARY CUTTING MATS

These are used in conjunction with a rotary cutter. See pages 33, Notions, and 113, 114, High Leg Teddy, for illustrations on use of rotary cutting mats.

CUTTING TIPS

1. Pre-shrink fabric (see page 22).

2. Press your pattern to remove wrinkles.

3. Lay fabric on cutting board and pin selvedges together if cutting double. Use the flannelette **underside of a vinyl tablecloth** if you need extra holding power.

4. Check the grain frequently as silk loves to move. If possible, have the fabric store "rip" your silk. This ensures that the ends are straight and eliminates the need to pull a thread to straighten the goods.

5. Follow pattern layout. If you wish to cut on the bias refer to Chapter 18 – Cutting on the bias, page 84. If using satins on the straight grain, it is advisable to use **With Nap – one way** direction, layout.

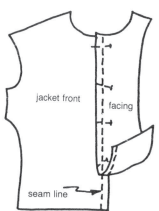

6. Eliminate seams where possible. If not needed for styling effect, some seams can be cut on the fold. Cut the front facing of a dress or suit all in one with the front of garment. This gives less bulk and a smooth edge. This technique is usually only suitable for straight edges and requires a bit more fabric. The final result can be worth it in your professionally finished garment!

7. If using shears, place quite a few pins on pattern, use one hand to secure the fabric while cutting with the other. Use long strokes to cut fabric.

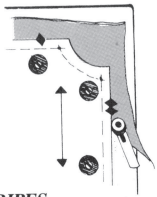

8. If using **Rotary Cutter** place a plastic ruler beside long straight edges. Ensure that you have cutting surface beneath. Weights may be used as there is no fabric or pattern movement with this method. Plastic tacks may be used with some rotary mats. Try on sample fabric scrap to ensure tacks will not make holes.

STRIPES

With silk, I prefer to cut stripes **SINGLE** thickness. This is made easier by tracing off a full front or full back as flipping the pattern over is not nearly as accurate. This is more time consuming but the effort is more reliable in achieving stripes that match perfectly.

Uneven Stripes

HORIZONTAL – this layout is essentially the same as even stripes providing you use the "with nap" directions or have the pattern pieces running the same direction.

Variations

DROPPED SHOULDER STYLES – have the main body of the garment running vertically and the sleeves horizontally. Put the patch pockets running opposite to the direction of the body of the garment. Run panels and yokes in opposite directions for an interesting effect. Buttonhole pockets can be cut on the bias. Try a bias stripe, cap sleeve blouse. See Lingerie, page 84.

If you wish to use your pattern over again as a basic, or if it is a multiple sized pattern, trace it off using pattern tracing cloth or fuse it with iron-on non-woven interfacing which will preserve all the markings and pattern numbers.

MARKING METHODS

Snipping

This is probably the fastest method of marking for notches and darts on the seam allowance edges. Cut seam allowance edges straight (no joggs for the notches). Take tiny ⅛" snips in centre of notches. These will be cut off in serging or seam finishing.

Water Soluble Pens or Invisible Markers

Check your fabric to ensure that the marks will come out with water or evaporate in 48 hours. Choose a colour which is not too much of a contrast. It is wise to sew the darts right away if using the evaporating type marker.

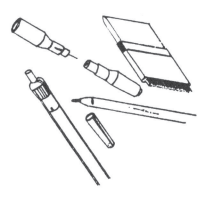

Pins

These are the safest of all for darts as you can transfer pin marks to wrong side with a very light marking pen or pencil.

Tailors Wax

This is not recommended for your lightweight silky fabrics as the wax will melt when heat is applied in ironing, leaving an oily mark.

I find my sewing goes much quicker if I cut out several garments at once, mark them and have them all ready for the sewing machine. If you use 48 hour evaporating marking pens, it could really speed up your sewing. Try it!

Linings

WHEN SHOULD I LINE A GARMENT?

Many of our synthetic fabrics do not require linings due to the density of the fabric and toughness of the fibres used in their manufacture. Putting the **stress of wear on the lining** is desirable with many silks, particularly Tussahs, some Duppionis and light weight types. While it is true that silk is very strong, the fabric itself may be loosely woven, creating the possibility of the threads pulling apart with wear. Using a skirt or dress lining will cut down on creasing at the hipline, as well as eliminate stretching in the seat area. A tailored jacket lining covers all the inner construction, making it easier to slip the garment over other fabrics, sweaters, etc. It will be extra work on your part but the extended life of the garment and continued good looks will be worth the effort. When any of the above are considerations take this as a cue to line your garment.

WHAT TYPE SHOULD I CHOOSE?

Pongee

This lightweight silk comes in a wide array of colours, is very soft and will mold nicely to any style. Would be ideal for lining dresses and light jackets. It is usually very inexpensive.

Bemberg Lining

This is my favourite lining for natural fibres. It is non-static and does not shrink. It will breath, making it a perfect summer or winter lining. Bemberg has a beautiful smooth silky hand. It is made from short fibres of rayon (regenerated cellulose -wood base). It comes in two widths 45″ (115 cm) or 54″ (137 cm) and is available in a large colour range.

> Tape a small paper sack on the edge of your sewing table. A perfect catch-all for your snipped threads and seam or trim cuttings.

Acetate

There are several acetate linings on the market. This quality is somewhat crisp and therefore wrinkles more so than Bemberg. This fabric, being a natural fibre, also breathes. There are variable weights for suits or dresses. Purchase a weight compatible to your garment.

These are just a few suggested linings. There are several other silks; eg. China, Habutae which are classed as lining silks, but tend to be a bit crisp. Many are available in natural colour only.

LOOSE LINING

SKIRTS – Eliminate pleats if desired but add a slit for walking ease. Sew side seams, darts, zipper on garment. Reversing the side for zipper, sew side seams, darts, leaving zipper opening on lining. The finished side of the lining will then be next to your body (wrong sides of skirt and lining together). Hand sew lining to zipper seam allowances. Apply waistband treating lining and garment as one. Make hem on lining one inch (2.5 cm) shorter than skirt finished length.

DRESSES – On one-piece garments attach separate lining at neckline only, attaching by hand on zipper seam allowances if applicable, and hand sewing the armseye seam separately in order to give freedom of movement. This is best for light coloured garments. If you have a waistline seam you may choose to line only the skirt portion, if using a heavier fabric.

> Try lining only the sleeve on a jacket. The most difficult area to slide into is the sleeve area. This will give you a finished armhole seam as you can tack the lining over the raw edge.

PANT LINER

Make a separate pair of slacks from a durable lining fabric. If you intend to wear them with natural fibres you might consider Bemberg lining as it is strong, durable and will breath along with your outer garment. Polyester lining is also suitable but would not afford you these same qualit ies. Make it in a basic style suitable for wearing beneath any of your slacks. This will prolong the life of your pants, keep them in better shape, and your slacks will not need washing or cleaning as often. Nylon Tricot also can be used, but it would not preserve the shape of your slack in that it stretches on the crossgrain. It would be, how-ever, more comfortable to wear. If you would like to wear the pant liner as a pajama bottom you can add a lace trim.

UNDERLINING

The lining is sewn into the seams and treated as one fabric for construction with this method. There are a few problems that can develop unless the fabrics are totally compatible. If your outer fabric stretches and your lining doesn't you will have puckering at the seams with a droopey look to your outer garment. This does tend to give a somewhat bulky appearance. The safest method by far is loose lining.

PATCH POCKET LINING (with facing)

1. Take pocket pattern and fold down facing hem. Cut lining from lower edge of pocket to ½" (1.3 cm) above the bottom edge of facing. Trim lining ⅛" (3mm) on outer edges; (this eliminates lining showing to right side on finished pocket).

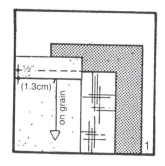 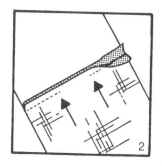

2. Stitch lining to pocket right sides together in a ¼" (6mm) seam leaving a small opening in centre for turning. Press seam open.

3. With right sides together bring bottom edges together and pin all around pocket. Stitch on seamline (⅝" or 1.5cm) side and bottom edges. Trim seams and corners or if making a rounded bottom notch out excess fabric on curved edges.

 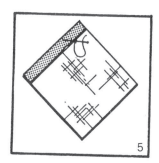

4. Using small opening on facing, carefully pull pocket to right side. Press pocket from lining side in order to ensure lining is pulling to underside of pocket.

5. Slipstitch facing opening closed.

POCKET FLAP LINING

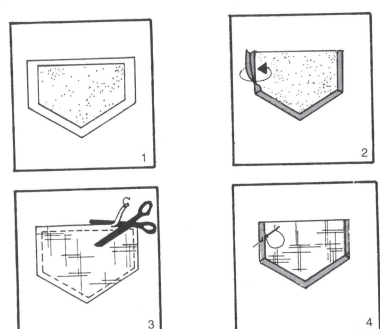

To reduce bulk in your flap:

1. Cut one flap of fabric and one of lining. Appropriately interface the flap.

2. Press under seam allowance, mitering corners if you wish (this will give a beautiful flat finish).

3. Cut ¼" (6mm) off outer edges of lining. Press to wrong side a ½" (1.3cm) seam. Key top raw edges and pin lining and flaps wrong sides together;

4. Slip stitch by hand the lining to the pocket. Apply flap at top of pocket as per pattern directions. This is a couture finish for that special garment!

Save the small scrap pieces of your crepe de chines and charmeuse fabrics. These are ideal to line your patch pockets.

Sewing Silks

You may worry that silk will be difficult to sew. I have found that in general it is one of the easiest! The slippery lightweight types will move but with practice and a few tips on eliminating this problem you will be well on your way to easier sewing with this fabric.

ADJUST YOUR SEWING MACHINE

Silks (especially fine ones) do not need a heavy pressure. There is a button or dial usually at the top of your machine which you can adjust to loosen the pressure on the pressure foot. You will also need to adjust the tension on a scrap of fabric to ensure that it is correct. The bobbin tension may need to be loosened.

TENSION IS CORRECT

BOTTOM TENSION TOO TIGHT

TOP TENSION TOO TIGHT

Even Feed Foot

This is built in to some machines but can be purchased as a separate attachment for others. This is extremely helpful for very light weight sheer fabrics along with the heavier ones as it keeps the seam flat, not allowing the top piece of fabric to be pushed or puckered.

Stitch Length

I have found that a slightly smaller stitch works best with your finer silks. Try a setting of 2 or 15 sts. per inch. The finer stitching is particularly suitable for narrow hems which can be double topstitched. See Hem Finishes, Page 73.

Puckered Seams

If you have adjusted your tension on the machine correctly, you should not have this problem. However, if you have done everything possible, you may try gently pulling both back and front of the needle while sewing. This is referred to as "taut" sewing.

PIECE OF FABRIC ON SEWING TABLE

Placing a piece of flannelette, muslin felt, or sportweight poly/cotton on your sewing table can eliminate the sliding of your garment while sewing. Pin fabric from underneath to hold in place.

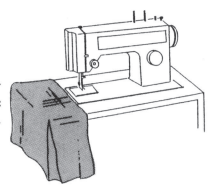

TISSUE PAPER

Placing tissue paper under seam can make for easier handling of fabric. Tear paper away after stitching.

OILING MACHINE

Do not oil just before beginning your silk project. Give yourself at least 24 hours and stitch through some other cloth scraps, wiping off any excess oil that might come in contact with your garment.

Serge Ends of loosely woven, ravelled fabric prior to washing and cutting out garment.

STARTING YOUR SEAM

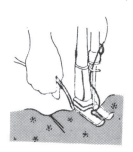

Pull threads from the back. This will eliminate the possibility of their going down into the race and getting tangled or worse yet, making a hole in your silk. Let this become a habit as any fine textured fabric will have this tendency. Backtack approximately ½" from edge when starting a seam.

STAY STITCHING

It is advisable to staystitch the neckedge on all garments, in order to maintain original shape while sewing the other sections. If you plan to try the garment on several times, the armhole edges should also be stay-stitched. Stitch with the grain of the fabric, like petting a cat! It is also advisable to use directional stitching when sewing the seams.

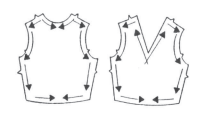

Pattern Folder

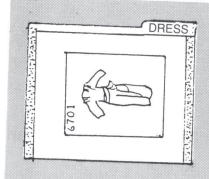

DRESS

6701

Take a letter sized file folder and tape the sides together. Glue the front and back of pattern envelope to file folder covers. This allows traced patterns to be reused and packed easily. Use a file box as a reference system for fashions and ideas.

Seam Finishes

The type of seam used to finish a garment will depend on the type of care the garment will have later (washing or drycleaning) and whether the seams will be shown during wearing. A cosmetic coat or karate robe would be best serged or french seamed. Some fabrics are very prone to fraying which would prompt the use of a serged or enclosed seam.

PLAIN SEAM

Generally a ⅝″ (1.5cm) seam allowance, sewn with straight stitch and pressed open. A second row of straight stitching can be sewn along edges of seam allowance. This seam is suitable for heavier fabrics for use with straight sewing machines.

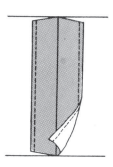

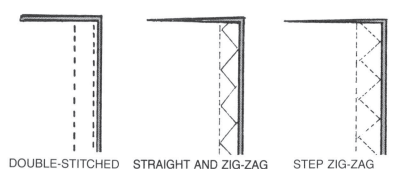

DOUBLE-STITCHED   STRAIGHT AND ZIG-ZAG   STEP ZIG-ZAG

DOUBLE-STITCHED SEAM

A strong, narrow variation of the plain seam. The seam allowance is usually trimmed to ¼″ (6mm) with the second row of straight stitching close to the edge of seam allowance. Use this method for garments which will not expose seams or where a pressed open, flat seam is not essential (blouses, lingerie, etc.).

STRAIGHT AND ZIG-ZAG

¼″ (6mm) seam allowance. Seam line is sewn with straight stitch with second row close to edge of seam allowance zig-zagged.

STEP ZIG-ZAG

Use step zig-zag stitch instead of plain zig-zag. This puckers much less than a regular zig-zag, on the lighter silks.

PINKED

A Pinked ⅝″ (1.5 cm) seam is always acceptable on silks and is less bulky than many of the seam finishes. It is actually more acceptable for people with only straight sewing machines. Cutting out directly with pinking shears will eliminate a separate step. A row of straight stitching close to pinked edge will re-inforce pinked edge against any possible fraying.

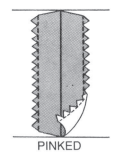

PINKED

TURNED AND STITCHED

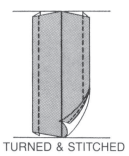

TURNED & STITCHED

Also called clean-finishing. Straight stitch ⅝″ (1.5 cm) seam. Turn under long straight edges ⅛″ (3mm) or ¼″ (6mm) and stitch close to folded edge. Some of the most expensive silk garments are finished with this seam type.

BLIND HEM STITCHED

Straight stitch ⅝″ (1.5cm) seam. Use blind hem stitch close to edge but not over as it will pucker. Trim close to stitching on under side.

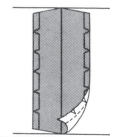

BLIND HEM STITCHED

HONG KONG FINISH

Similar to a bias bound finish but less bulky. Attractive on garments where the seams are exposed to view.

HONG KONG FINISH

1. Cut l½" (3.8cm) bias strips (see page 88, Cutting Bias) from a lining silk or similar weight in a contrast or matching colour.

2. Stitch bias strip to seam allowance edge in a ¼" (6cm) seam with right sides together.

3. Turn bias over edge to underside and press. From right side stitch in the well of the seam catching bias on underside. There is no need to finish raw edge on bias as it will not ravel. On a special garment you may want to do this last step by hand to give a softer finish, but it will be much more time consuming. This finish is a very attractive hem treatment for a an unlined jacket.

SHEER TRICOT BIAS SEAMS FINISH

This can be purchased as a notion item in a packaged roll. See Notions, Page 33 for information on applying to seam edges.

FRENCH SEAM

This is ideal for robes and sheer, lightweight silks when a completely concealed look is required. This seam is very durable and will handle well with washing. The seam is stitched once from the right side of the fabric and once from the wrong side. The narrower the finished seam the more attractive.

1. With wrong sides together stitch ⅜" from edge. Trim seam allowances to ⅛" (3cm). Press seam open (this step is purely to ease the folding back in the next step).

2. Fold right sides together with stitched edge exactly on top of fold. Stitch a ¼″ (6cm) seam enclosing raw edges of seam allowance. Be sure to keep this width of seam as a wider one gives a rather bulky look.

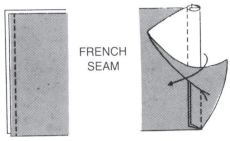

FRENCH SEAM

MOCK FRENCH SEAM

This seam works well on a curved edge such as an armhole seam. Stitch a normal ⅝″ (1.5cm) seam right sides together. Trim seam allowances to ½″ (1.3cm). Turn in seam edges ¼″ (6cm) and press, matching folded edges. Stitch these folded edges together.

MACHINE ROLLED HEM

This method can be used for finishing seam edges. Refer to Hem finishes, page 74 for instructions.

There are several other possible seam finishes such as a flat-felled seam, or the self-bound seam. These would work well on crisper silks, but the turning in on seam allowances on softer silks would be difficult. Refer to your regular sewing book if you wish to try these.

SERGING

Refer to the Overlock Serging Machines chapter 13. This can be the most time saving of all seam finishes. The speed and expertise achieved make it difficult to use anything else!

Overlock Serging Machines

In keeping with the innovative 80's we as homesewers are now able to maintain pace with manufacturing techniques available to us in the form of serging machines. These powerful little machines will sew up to 1700 stitches per minute. They not only stitch but will trim and overcast all in **ONE** efficient operation. Have you often wished you could finish your seams as in store bought garments? Now you can!

There are several basic types of sergers for specific needs. You need to decide which type of sewing you will be doing most, prior to making your purchase. The types described as follows cover the most popular at this writing.

THREE THREAD SERGER

This machine is an overlock stitching serger using three threads. It can be used to sew seams, giving an elastic stitch very suitable for knits and garments needing some ease. Bias cut garments fit into this category. There are several features that vary from machine to machine including, flat locking, some convert to a two- stitch finish if desired, some have a built-in light and others will stitch a tiny rolled hem with or without changing the throat plate.

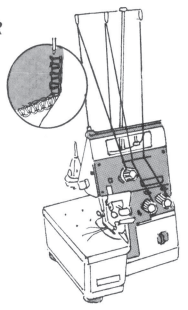

3 THREAD OVERLOCK

THREE/FOUR THREAD SERGER

This machine will basically stitch the same as the three-thread but adds an additional row of straight stitching down the middle, for added strength. This is formed by a second needle which runs parallel to the first, similar to a twin needle. It has almost as much stretch to the stitch as the straight three-thread. This heavier stitching is not required for seam finishing only, therefore it is possible to remove one of the needles to give a lighter finish. This machine cannot convert to a two-thread machine, but it will do a rolled hem.

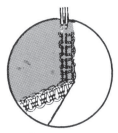

3/4 THREAD OVERLOCK

FOUR THREAD SERGER

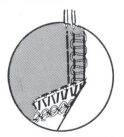

TRUE 4 THREAD OVERLOCK

Seam finishing for easily ravelled fabrics is simplified with this machine. The chain formed by two of the threads produces a very strong stitch. It is possible to drop the right needle and obtain a straight chain stitch, or drop the left needle and create an overedge stitch.

This four-thread stitching is not as elastic as the previous two types and generally has a much more bulky seam. It is not possible to do a rolled hem with this machine.

TWO/THREE/FOUR THREAD SERGER

This model is the newest machine to hit the marketplace. It will give you all the features of the previously mentioned machines. It has three loopers and therefore is a bit more complicated to thread. One of the these machines does have an easy threading looper system. This machine could be rather complicated for a beginner sewer to master, so unless you understand the workings of a serger, less options may be better.

PIN FIT

Machine or hand basting is still necessary as a last resort if using slippery or unusual fabric. However, this step gives a great opportunity for **fitting the garment** prior to final sewing! With serging, you cannot add to the seam allowance once the seam is cut.

PIN FIT

SEAMS

Decide ahead whether you wish a **regular straight seam with over-edge finishing** or a **stitched and cut overlock seam**. It is best to start with a ⅝″ (1.5cm) seam allowance when serging a narrow seam, trimming off excess when stitching.

OVEREDGE FINISH

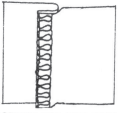

STITCHED AND CUT

A narrow **rolled** or **unrolled** seam is fabulous for sheer georgettes, tulle, and lace garments. The seam is so tiny that it seems to almost blend into the fabric. It is achieved by changing the throatplate or presser foot. The width of

ROLLED EDGE   UNROLLED EDGE

the stitch finger determines the width of the stitch. The **stitch length** will cause the stitch to be either solid (satin type) or spaced apart. A two or three-thread **picot edge** is a rolled edge with longer stitch length, created with this same stitch finger. Your serger book supplied with the machine will tell you how to set your machine for this stitch. The tiny little rolled edges are perfect for ruffles, lingerie hems, and scarves. Decorative effects by the addition of silky contrasting coloured threads add interest for special garments.

A serger opens up a whole new world of sewing. The speed and time saved in garment construction is phenomenal! To sew your lingerie, T-shirts, and regular clothing in half the usual time gives renewed interest in sewing to many half-hearted seamstresses, as well as enabling advanced sewers to produce many more professionally finished garments. Once you have mastered the threading, tension adjustments and general operation of a serger you will want to use it more and more.

Sergers do not replace your regular sewing machine.

Although it is possible to sew a complete garment (some are advertised as the 10 minute dress!) you will still need to use your conventional sewing machine for a pressed open seam, installing zippers, topstitching and buttonholes.

I am not taking the time to explain all the details of serger operation. There are several excellent publications available at this writing which cover the aspects of serger sewing in greater detail (with step by step instructions and graphic illustrations for ease in learning). Our **COUTURE ACTION KNITS** revised book covers the majority of techniques for sewing with sergers. The applications can also be applied to silk and satin fabrics.

> ***Serger Tip:*** When finishing a serger seam end, take a crochet hook or look turner and put tail back inside your finished serged seam. The tiny crochet hooks are very quick and easy to use. If desired, a seams sealant such as Fray Check can be used instead, trimming off excess chain after it is dried.

Pressing

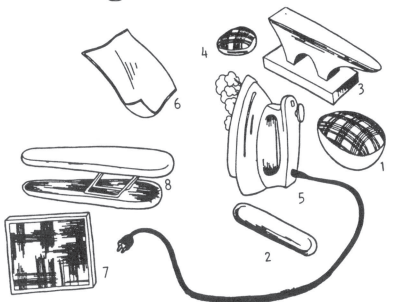

"Pressing as you sew" is the key to a **professional** looking garment. However, over-pressing creates a worn look. Most silks do not require heavy pressing, except for some of the suiting types. Press seams open as you stitch, but handle the top-pressing with care. It is best to use a press cloth to avoid shiny spots after pressing. The following pressing items will make your work easier:

1. ***Tailor's Ham:*** Oval style in shape to give those areas such as darts, curved areas, neck openings the contour needed for that professional appearance.

2. ***Seam Roll:*** Long cylindrical roll primarily used in pressing seams so edges do not show through. Use in pressing narrow sleeve seams and pant legs.

3. ***Point Presser:*** Very helpful in pressing seams open in corners such as collars and tabs. A Clapper is often part of this unit (forming a base) which assists in retaining steam in seam to help flatten.

4. **Press Mitt:** This padded mitt slips into hard to reach areas or under the garment for a light steam press from right side in final touch up and finish. It can be slipped over end of sleeve board.

5. **Steam Iron:** The newer, shot of steam irons are excellent. The more holes the better. If you have a drippy iron, a new one could be a wise investment prior to sewing your first silk project. Generally the Permanent Press setting is best for silks.

6. **Press Cloths:** Light weight, see-thru press cloths are best. Old diapers make excellent press cloths too! Cotton Batiste is excellent along with the see-thru purchased types. The woven rather than non-woven types are best.

7. **Velvaboard:** Ideal for velvets and corduroy fabrics as it has bristles on the pad which lift fabric and thus avoid crushing while pressing.

8. **Sleeveboard:** Used for pressing sleeves and other hard to reach hems (e.g. cuffs). Can be used with press mitts, placed over board end.

> **NOTE:** Silicone finishes on Ironing Board covers do not allow the steam to penetrate into the garment. Sometimes the finish will come off leaving gold or silver specks on your garment. Cotton makes the best cover.

Write needle number sizes in each section of a tomatoe pin cushion (white marking pencil works well). When you need to change needles if not well used, place in the respective spot.

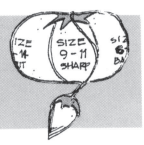

DART PRESSING

Darts should be sewn with regular stitch to within ½″ (1.3cm) of end. Change at that point to a tiny stitch running off end of dart and letting the threads twist. Cut the ends leaving a ½″ (1.3cm) tail. Press dart (from wrong side), folded edge flat in the same position as stitched. This will help to smooth stitching.

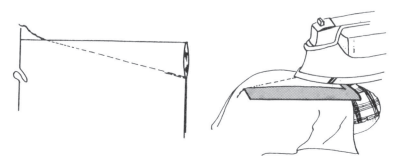

Place garment and dart over a ham. Place dart end at ham end and press dart down if horizontal or to center for vertical darts. Placing a piece of brown paper under dart will eliminate a line showing through. Turn to right side and top press, using a press cloth. If dart edge still shows through return to the underside and press on garment side, steaming out line.

Caution! Perfume can be very destructive to silk fibres, causing dyes to fade. For best results, apply your perfume before putting on garment.

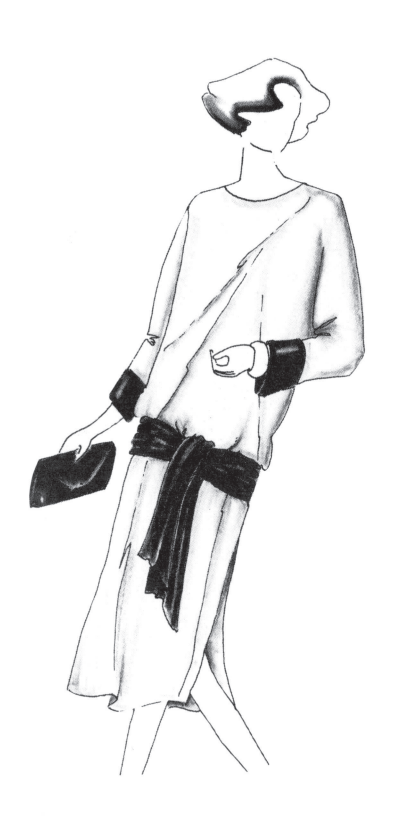

Zippers

Choose the lightest weight zipper possible. Some have nylon tapes and are excellent for the finer lightweight silks. Suiting weight silks can handle regular zippers. Try the following method for installing a regular lapped zipper.

REGULAR LAPPED APPLICATION

1. Must have at least ⅝″ (1.5cm) seam allowance (¾″/2cm is better). Measure and mark exact length of placket opening using zipper (with pull tab up), plus seam allowance. Mark this length on garment seam. Stitch seam closed with regular stitching, backtack, then change to a long basting stitch for zipper placket.

2. Press open seam and remove the basting stitches in placket area by clipping bottom stitch and pulling from the top.

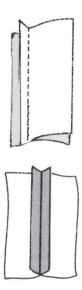

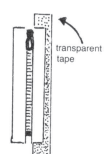

transparent tape

3. Position a piece of "magic transparent tape" to cloth edge on right-hand side of zipper back. Half of tape edge extends beyond zipper tape.

4. Working from right side, place folded edge of garment opening close to zipper teeth, pressing the tape to back of seam allowance. The tape holds zipper in position acting as basting.

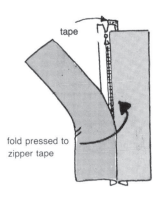

tape

fold pressed to zipper tape

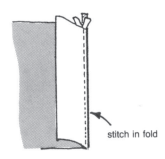

stitch in fold

5. Using zipper foot, turn up seam allowance and sew in fold from right side (pressed crease). To start sewing, pull zipper tab slightly down, leaving needle in fabric, while you pull it up when you reach the tab. **No stitches are visible on the right side** with this in-the-fold sewing method.

If desired, you may sew on right side of fabric close to zipper teeth rather than by above method. Sewing from behind is by far the nicest method for finer silks and dressier fabrics.

6. Place the folded edges together, on right side, overlapping slightly to hide zipper. Tape the edges together. Topstitch ¼" (6mm) to ⅜" (1cm) over from folded edge, through all thicknesses (use zipper foot) starting from the bottom. When you reach tab, release tape; pull tab down and carefully finish stitching to top. **PRESTO!! A completed zipper without basting!**

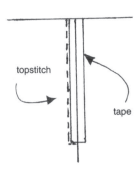

topstitch

tape

PRICKSTITCH

7. Hand topstitching on final step gives your garment a couturier look. Use a tiny, prick stitch. Insert needle through all layers to right side. Reinsert a few threads behind and bring up approximately ¼" (6mm) ahead of first stitch. To give added strength you may sew a row of machine stitching behind, joining seam allowance and zipper tape together. This zipper finish is very attractive for your lightweight silk fabrics.

CENTERED APPLICATION

Usually used in the center back of a garment. Follow Step 1 and 2 of the lapped application, with the following changes:

2. Do not remove basting stitches.

3. Rub washable glue stick on right sides of zipper tape. Place zipper face down on seam allowance. Press for glue to hold.

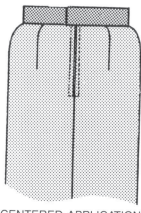

CENTERED APPLICATION

4. Place a strip of magic tape the width desired (usually ¾" /2cm) on right side as guide for topstitching.

5. Topstitch either by machine or hand, using the prickstitch.

6. Remove basting stitches.

Hem Finishes

Your choice of hem can either blend with the garment or be a noticeable feature, depending on the weight of the fabric.

INVISIBLE MACHINE HEM

Fold up hem and fold back on itself allowing ¼"(6mm) or more to extend up from hemside. Use a regular zig-zag catching every second or third stitch on garment fold. If you have built-in blind hemmer, use that along with the special foot which has a guide for the fold of fabric. You may wish to finish the raw edge by turning over and top-stitching prior to stitching the invisible hem, particularly on light weight silks. This hem is very durable for garments that will be washed continuously. The hem stitching on fine fabrics often is quite noticeable.

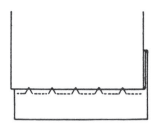

NARROW MACHINE STITCHED HEM

This is suitable for cap-sleeve edges, blouse bottoms and even dress or robe hems. Leave a ½"(1.3cm) hem allowance. Turn under ¼" (6mm) and press. Turn again ¼" (6mm) and stitch close to hem edge using small stitches (15 sts. to inch or 2 on European machines). I like to add an additional row of stitching along the bottom fold of hem. Look at ready-to-wear silks and you will notice they often have two rows of stitching.

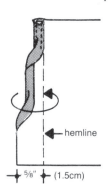

hemline

⅝"   (1.5cm)

A variation of this is to use a twin needle and sew two rows of stitching all in one operation. The rows of stitching, however, are extremely close together. See Footnote page 74

MACHINE ROLLED HEM

This is great for finishing fuller skirts, belt edges and ruffles. Suitable for lightweight silks. Use the rolled hemmer foot which normally comes with your machine. It gives almost a handkerchief hem. It is a very quick finish but the catch is getting started at the edge. Rolled heming can be done by hand using a tiny running stitch but it is very time consuming.

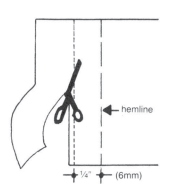

hemline

¼"   (6mm)

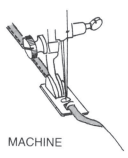

MACHINE

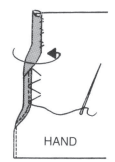

HAND

Double Topstitching narrow machine-stitched hems - follow method on page 73, stitching hem edge first. Prior to stitching second row, with double threaded needle, take a couple tiny stitches at outer point of corner, leaving 3" (7.6cm) tails (no knot). With machine topstitch to corner and pivot. Holding threads securely

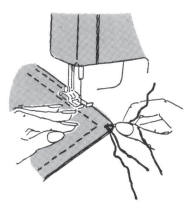

with other hand, begin sewing again. This will eliminate puckering which very often occurs on front corners or slits when adding this additional row of stitching on bottom edge.

BLIND CATCH STITCH HEM

This is my favourite traditional handstitched hem. Finish the hem edge with either turning in ¼″(6mm) and topstitching on lighter silks, using straight or multiple zig-zag stitch. If you have a serger, finish with serging. Seam binding can be used if you wish, but leave it loose on top, apply to hem edge and then proceed as follows:

Turn up a hem width and then fold back ¼″ (6mm) hem edge toward yourself on wrong side. Work from left to right with needle pointing left. Make a catch stitch (resembles cross stitch) underneath this area. **IMPORTANT!** Keep this stitch loose and pick up one thread **ONLY** on the garment side. **Do NOT pull tight**, so it won't show, or break as you walk or move, as it needs to have some built-in "give". Leaving the ¼″ (6mm) hem above top fold allows the option of running an iron between hem and garment which eliminates a ridge showing.

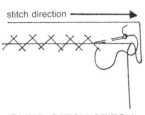

stitch direction ⟶

BLIND CATCH STITCH

HEMS WITH BOX OR KNIFE PLEATS

Stitch pleat seam to within 5 or 6 inches (12.5 to 15 cm) of hem edge. Finish hem as desired. Then finish pleat seams, stitching through the finished hem. This method gives a flat lying pleat. If desired, folded pleat edge can be topstitched through all layers from waist down.

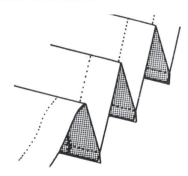

Which hem should I use? Personal rule of thumb is to use a machine hem if garment is to be washed. If it will be drycleaned a hand sewn hem is less conspicuous and elegant in appearance.

Buttonholes

BOUND BUTTONHOLES are not normally found on many manufactured garments. Often the only available places are very expensive couture type clothing or specialty boutiques. This does not mean bound buttonholes are passe' but rather labour costs in the garment industry have made it time-prohibitive to put these on most clothing.

As a homesewer you have the time to put professional touches into your sewing. These buttonholes are meant for the dressmaker suits and dresses, and are usually not put on a tailored blazer style jacket. I find them easier and more fool-proof than machine buttonholes, giving a very lovely finish to your silk jackets and dresses. It takes approximately one-half hour to do two buttonholes from start to finish. If you are afraid to tackle them let me challenge you to follow these simple steps and make a sample. I'm sure you'll agree how easy it can be!

BUTTONHOLE PLACEMENT

Horizontal buttonhole should begin ⅛″ (3mm) over center front line toward garment edge. Button shank will then sit in center position.

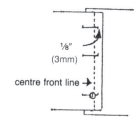

BUTTONHOLE LENGTH

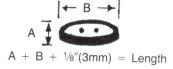

A + B + ⅛″(3mm) = Length

Measure button diameter plus thickness and add ⅛″ (3mm) to measurement.

BOUND BUTTONHOLES give a "couture" look to firmer fabrics. They require a fabric that has some body. Crepe de Chines and Charmeuse would not be suitable, but silk linens, duppionis, shantungs and suiting silks of all types lend themselves beautifully.

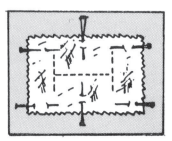

1. Place a piece of sheer fabric (right sides together) on garment body. Cotton organdy (preshrunk) or polyester organza work well. Mark buttonhole directly on the sheer fabric (use newer fabric marking pen or pencil).

2. Stitch around the buttonhole box using a smaller stitch. When reaching the corner of box area ensure needle is down in fabric before pivoting. Then count stitches to each end to ensure even box size.

3. Cut all thicknesses through the center of box to within ⅜" (1cm) of each end. Clip diagonally into each corner forming pie shaped pieces. Be careful not to cut through your stitches.

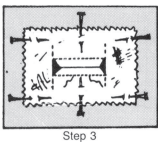
Step 3

Step 4

4. Pull sheer fabric to underside. Ensure the sheer is not visible from box front. Press. Place a dob of "Sobo" glue or washable glue stick (this would be best for lighter suit silks) on the wrong side of sheer fabric on each side of box.

5. Cut two pieces of fabric on the bias 2½"(6.5cm) by 2" (5cm). Place right sides together, divide in half widthwise, sew basting stitch down centre line.

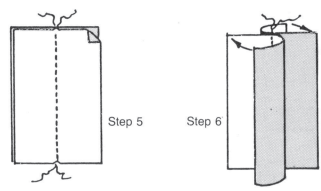

Step 5　　　Step 6

6. Spread open like book pages; bring wrong sides together. The center stitching will not be visible.

7. Center box area over the center of patch. Press garment and patch together with fingers, where glue was used. Turn upper piece back and expose the long tab. Stitch lip in place with short stitches, sewing on top of previous stitching. Do both sides.

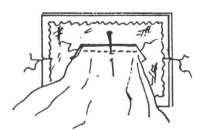
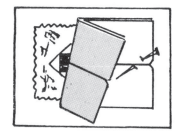

Sew pie-shaped end pieces last. You will be sewing through **all** thicknesses.

Trim excess buttonhole fabric grading seam in a circular shape to prevent corners from showing through to garment right side.

8. Remove the basting holding lips together. The separation will form the lips of buttonhole.

9. For a neater facing side repeat steps 1 through 4 and slip stitch the two sides together, or poke pins through to the facing side from the front ends of buttonhole. Slash between pins and carefully tuck in raw edge and hand sew edges, (Next page).

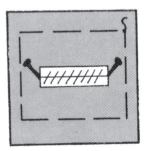

right side

wrong side

Corded Bound Buttonhole

If you would like to have the lips on the buttonhole padded, insert preshrunk string or crochet cotton prior to sewing ends of buttonhole in Step 7.

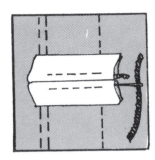

MACHINE BUTTONHOLES

Ensure facing area is interfaced to give stability. Mark guidelines for sewing buttonhole with a basting thread or water soluble marking pens. Test on fabric scrap first.

Which direction should I put the buttonholes?

VERTICAL BUTTONHOLES are normally placed on shirt plackets, and bands. They require smaller buttons and are placed on the centre front line.

HORIZONTAL BUTTONHOLES are more secure and used on most items of clothing. See Bound Buttonhole section for size and placement of buttonholes. Some machines do not have built in buttonholers. If that is the case a universal buttonhole attachment will do the trick. Use the clear buttonhole foot which comes with your machine or a special marked buttonhole foot for gauging the size easily. A machine basting stitch will also give proper guidelines. The new computerized machines have amazing features. You program in the size of your first buttonhole and it will automatically do each successive buttonhole the same size. It is very important to make sure that the interfacing is the same thickness throughout, as well as no seam interference, as these will throw off the computer and you will not achieve uniformity in size. The fabric must also be smooth as a textured fabric will have high-low sections and again the messages transmitted to the computer will be confusing. All computer machines can work a buttonhole manually so you may need to do this in several of the above situations. In order to give stability to sewing fine fabrics you may want to put a piece of stitch and tear behind and remove it after stitching the buttonholes.

Slit the buttonhole down the centre. There are special buttonhole scissors which have a protector to keep from snipping through the stitching.

Should you cut a thread, return to the machine and zig-zag slightly, or you may use Fray Check, being very careful to put the liquid on the edge of the buttonhole only.

Test on a scrap piece of fabric first.

Corded Machine Buttonholes

If your machine has a special buttonhole foot with a little hook on the back, you may loop a piece of buttonhole twist or fine cord around this and proceed to sew as usual. After the buttonhole is sewn, pull the cord, taking out any ripple or slack in buttonhole. Snip cords, and flatten buttonhole. Pulled cords will recede under stitching after they are snipped. This extra cord will keep button-hole from stretching aside from giving it a nice rounded effect.

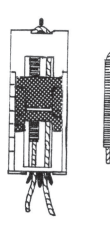

Bias Tubing Buttonholes

See Special Treatments, page 115.

HIDDEN PLACKET

This is a beautiful, simple finish for silk a dress or blouse with collar. If well finished buttonholes are difficult to achieve, they are neatly tucked underneath with this method. Choose this style for your next blouse and you'll be pleasantly surprised at how easy buttonholes can be!

It is easier to stitch a straight seam if you stitch the zig-zag or seam closest to seam allowance first and then straight stitch the seam line.

Lingerie

> " Whenas in silks my Julia goes,
> Then, then, methinks how sweetly flows
> That liquefaction of her clothes"
>
> Robert Herrick
> 17th Century English Poet

NIGHT AND DAY INTIMATES

Our concentration in this section will be to introduce you to the wonderful world of satiny sensations and ultimate luxury of silk and lingerie.

Following the Victorian era and the simplification of our undergarments, the creation of luscious lightweight lingerie has been made available to even a beginner seamstress. An enticing collection of free flowing silks and shimmering polyester delicacies can be seen in any lingerie department. Avail yourself of these "free idea shows" by browsing and checking out the techniques as applied to these garments. Lingerie, sleepwear sections in pattern catalogues include designs for the new trendy "sleep-shirts", teddies, camisole-tap pants, slips and nighties. Some are suitable for stretchy knits only, so check the pattern envelopes.

To cast aside your ever faithful flannelette gown may be somewhat traumatic, but let me encourage you to experience the thoroughly feminine flattery as you take off on a "flight of fantasy" in silk!

In the early 1900's, French Designer Madeleine Vionnet, discovered garments flowed, clung smoothly over the body and swirled with motion by cutting on the bias.

This expanded a whole new world to the fashion scene. To give the comfort desired for your delicate underwear when working with woven fabrics, bias will be the desired method of cutting.

CUTTING ON THE BIAS

When should I cut on the Bias?

Bias cut garments flatter any body figure, giving your fashions a fluid, body-clinging look. Many regular dress styles can be cut on the bias, but normally if a garment is styled for that look the pattern will specify cutting on the bias. Sometimes entire garments are cut on the bias, or bias may be used sectionally for design purposes, such as skirt or blouse front panels. Yokes are often cut on the bias when using stripes or plaids to create an interesting effect. Remember, bias will stretch so the placement within a garment could affect the hang and the overall appearance. The "give" afforded by bias makes it especially suited to any close-fitting lingerie styles, such as camisoles, teddies, panties or nighties. It is not necessary to cut robes or garments with gathers and fullness on the bias as they do not require ease in molding to the body.

SIZING

The bust area often requires more give. If you are C-Cup or bigger in this area buy a pattern one size larger.

FABRIC SELECTION

Bias cut garments work best wih softly finished, drapey fabrics. Crepe de chine, Charmeuse, Satin, Chiffon, Georgette, are some that lend themselves well to this styling. **Unlined garments** are recommended as difference of elasticity may vary between outer garment and lining.

SELVEDGE

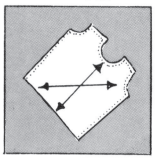

BIAS PLACEMENT

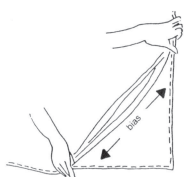

True bias is a 45 degree angle to any straight edge when grains are perpendicular. Fabric cut on true bias has maximum "give". This may eliminate the need for darts and shaping usually required when using the straight grain.

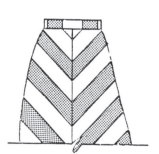

WIDEST WIDTH BEST

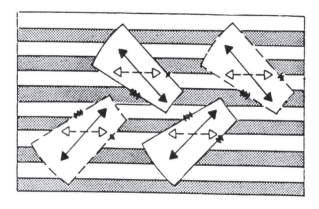

If you have a choice, purchase widest fabric, for making bias cut garments. If changing from lengthwise grain to bias, you will need to layout your pattern on an imaginary width using your floor or table in order to determine the amount of fabric needed. A cutting board with 1″ (2.5cm) marking makes this easier. It does take more fabric!

TIPS ON CUTTING BIAS

1. Bias cut edges will not fray. No seam finishing is required except for appearance sake and regular shears or cutters can be used.

2. Use a large, non-slippery surface for cutting, ensuring your fabric does not hang over the table. Refer to Step 4 or 5, Layout and Cutting Chapter, page 45.

3. Rotary Cutting tools are ideal for bias. Fabric has a tendency to move and stretch, when using scissors. The fabric lifts producing "wows" along the edges. Use lots of pins to hold the fabric pieces together if scissors are used. Wider seam allowances are advisable as garment will stretch and you may wish a bit more width. These can always be trimmed if not needed. Mark carefully prior to moving cut garment pieces from table. See Layout and Cutting Chapter, page 45.

4. Hang garment pieces over a rounded hangar for at least 24 hours prior to seaming. **This is a very important step** as edges will stretch and your seam would hang unevenly if omitted.

SEWING BIAS

On longer lengthwise seams, it is advisable to loosely hand-baste seam and let hang overnite prior to sewing. This loose basting allows garment to slide to it's normal wearing length.

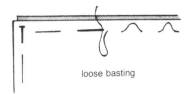

loose basting

To avoid seams breaking with stress, during wear, use a smaller stitch than normal. Use a silk, cotton wrapped polyester or polyester thread. But **DO NOT USE PURE COTTON**!

The term "holding in" is the technique required while sewing necklines, sleeve edges and bias pockets. See Fast Fitting Tips, page 42.

When sewing a **bias-to-straight fabric seam**, take special care in not stretching the bias edge, to avoid rippling. Pin baste every 2 or 3 inches (5 to 7.5cm) sewing with the **bias edge on top** removing the pins as you stitch. This would apply to joining a bias skirt to the waistband.

TAPING SEAM

Tape any seam that you wish to stabilize; the shoulder would be one such area. You may use hem seam binding (preshrunk if not a polyester) or twill tape. Cut tape the length of shoulder shown on pattern piece and pin in place, stitching into the seam as you sew.

Zippers may cause a problem if proper care not taken to ensure the seam allowance isn't stretched while installing. A rippling or poking out can result. If desired, the back skirt sections only of a garment can be cut on the straight grain. This would tend to eliminate this problem. The centre back seam is the flattest location and a centered application with a hand prick-stitch for the top-stitching is advisable. See Zippers, page 70.

Hem your garment following a hanging period of 2 or 3 days. Use a hem marker, measuring up from the floor, evenly all around. Bias will be up and down and may need straightening. A narrow hem is advisable.

BIAS STRIPS

Bias Binding and Piping

1. Fold fabric diagonally so that a straight edge on the crosswise grain is parallel to the lengthwise grain (selvedge). Pin along top edges. Cut along the diagonal fold. Remove pins and the top fabric piece.

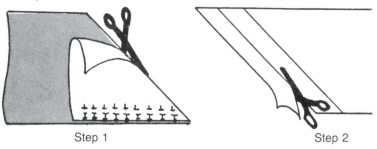

Step 1   Step 2

2. Draw a chalk or pencil line in the width desired, parallel to the diagonal edge. The most common widths for bias binding are 1″ (25mm) or 2″ (48mm). Draw as many lines as needed. Cut along lines, if only cutting one strip. For more than one see step 4.

Step 3

3. Place two strips together wrong sides out, so that the strips form a V shape. Align the seam lines letting the point extend beyond the edge of seamline. Machine stitch ¼″ (6mm) seam.

4. To join several strips at once, mark all strips, trim off the excess on the corners.

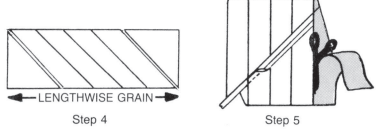

LENGTHWISE GRAIN

Step 4   Step 5

5. Fold fabric right sides together into a tube; aligning markings. Leave one strip width extending beyond seam width at each end. Stitch ¼" (6mm) seam.

6. Starting at one end begin cutting along marked line continuing until you reach opposite end.

BIAS TRIMMING AND TAPE MAKER

This under-rated notion item is one of the greatest inventions to hit the market. In the lingerie field, there are many ways to use these neat trims, made with your own matching fabric. They come in several widths, with the narrowest giving a fabulous dainty finish to cami-tap sets, nighties, etc.

1. Cut the cloth to width as specified on your tape maker instructions. Join pieces to give the length needed. Proceed now with the tape-maker.

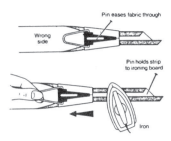

2. Feed the bias-cut fabric through the wide end of tape-maker, and press the folded binding as pulled through. If you have trouble pushing it into tape-maker, take a long needle to help poke bias through. Adjust iron to temperature of fabric type.

3. Fold tape over with one edge slightly wider than the other. This will ensure that while you are stitching it onto garment the wider edge (which is put underneath) will be caught in the stitching.

This bias trim can be used as an alternative to facings, necklines - round and V-neck; seam finishes; hem edges and casings.

SHAPING BIAS

If using bias in a curved area you will need to shape it prior to attaching. If binding is to be folded in half do this prior to shaping. Using a steam iron and the tip of the iron to hold bias, stretch and mold the opposite edge in a curve. As each section is shaped steam entire bias gently in place.

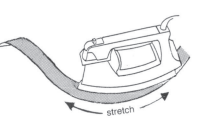

JOINING BIAS

It is difficult to pre-cut the desired length for an opening, as bias is stretchy. It is best to sew to within 2″ of meeting bias pieces. Cut excess trim away leaving a ¼″ (6mm) seam allowance on both ends. These cuts must be made on the straight of grain or angled line to alleviate bulk in the seam.

Fold and press top piece under ¼″ (6mm) on straight grain. Place over other end and pin. Continue stitching across join. Slip-stitch the joining if desired. Be careful to place the bias trim joins in an inconspicuous spot; the back or shoulder seam, etc.

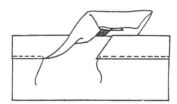

BIAS TUBING

1. Cut true bias strips as per previous section. Cut approximate length as required for garment. For spaghetti straps - a 1⅛" (3mm) width gives the narrow type strap.

2. Take one end and pin to end of ironing board or padded cutting board. Stretch and press piece, with steam iron, as much as possible. Pin other end to board and let dry. This elinates stretching later, while wearing.

3. Fold in half lengthwise and stitch using small stitches, ¼"(6mm) from fold, stretching bias as you sew. Seam allowances fill the tube so do not trim.

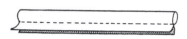

4. Using **loop turner** turn bias to right side. Latch hook is pushed through tube and hooked to end of fabric.

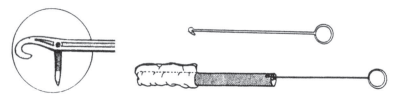

LOOP TURNER

Ease the fabric end through, while gently pulling the loop turner. And presto! This is ideal for the narrow tubing. Keeping pressure on the ring while pulling through will eliminate the hook from releasing in the middle of tube. You may have someone hold it or put your foot on the ring. Gauge your width of bias and take the same steps, if you desire wider tubing.

Corded Tubing can be made by threading a cord into finished tube. This is better for belts, drawstrings, etc.

BUTTONHOLE LOOPS

Place bias tubing as above, on garment right side, the size required. Use magic transparent tape to hold in place. Loops face toward garment. Place facing on top and stitch seam. These can be substituted on garments where the closing will be opened frequently, as thread loops are more difficult to unfasten.

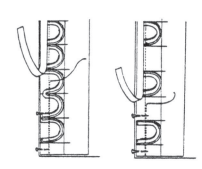

See Special Treatments, page 123 for frogs.

STITCHES BEST SUITED

Lingerie is one area where using a **serger** is fantastic! The simplicity of seaming, elasticity and durability will be appreciated. The tiny rolled hems are perfect for camisoles, tap pants, ruffles, etc. Use a shiny embroidery thread in the upper looper and you will have a beautiful decorative roll. Regular serger seam finishing is so attractive that you never need worry if it shows. The only area that you may use your regular sewing machine is in the application of lace and your straps.

I prefer two rows of top-stitching, one near the folded edge and one on the hem edge, using a small stitch and silk thread.

Any of the seam finishes from page 58 are suitable. Bear in mind the type of wear you will be giving the garment in question. If you will be washing your garment frequently you may want an enclosed or double-stitched seam. A kimono robe would be nicest with enclosed seams and possibly a machine hem. A robe sometimes hangs better with a wider hem so you might check that first.

If using nylon tricot, a tiny zig-zag stitch works best with narrow seams. Refer to **Couture Action Knits** book. The fabric will automatically roll over the edge to give it a finished look.

SHELL STITCH

This is one of the nicest stitches to finish the edges of lingerie. It is basically a blind hem stitch put in the machine from the opposite direction. If you tighten the top tension slightly it pulls in even more giving a scalloped look. I prefer to use a rolled hem to finish the raw edge for woven fabrics, along with this scalloped stitch . This edge finish is especially nice for pure silk satins as the beauty of the fabric does not require a lot of lace to create a soft romantic look. Remember the K.I.S.S. theory!

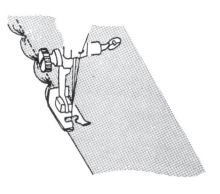

Applique Antique Hanky or Tablecloth Lace - For your next lingerie project consider the use of some of these beautiful laces. Join several together to achieve a pleasing effect. Even old tablecloths can be used for a "heritage" garment. Browse in a few Antique shops and old clothing places to find these treasures.

Lace Types

Lace has been a creation of the centuries. What an interesting experience it was to visit some of the oldest mills in Nottingham, England several years ago. Some of the lace books dated back to 1700! The intricacies and production on machinery in the 20th century is extremely fascinating. Each type of stitch is coded and put onto a graph by a draftsman who then gives it to another department for this to be transferred onto a punched card. This is then put onto a lace machine which begins to produce the lace. There are many different types of lace. Following are some of the major ones which you may refer to:

Acetate Lace

Rarely is acetate produced totally on it's own without the addition of polyester or nylon and occasionally cotton. Acetate tends to go limp if washed in too hot water and does not have the wearability of nylon and polyester. However, some of the silky threads that are put in lace must be acetate to give the shiny appearance. If the blend is good this can be a nice addition. Usually acetate quality laces are much cheaper.

All-Over Lace Yardage

Lace yardage is the type that you would make a complete garment. It comes in widths ranging from 90 cm (36″) up to 150 cm (60″). The contents will vary from nylon, polyester, acetate, cotton and many are blended together. The detail in the patterning and quality will govern the price.

You may use either lengthwise or crosswise grain depending on whether you wish to incorporate a scalloped edge. All of the lace types below are available in both edgings and all-overs.

Cluney Lace

This hand-crocheted looking lace comes in both cotton and polyester. It is nice in vintage looking garments and curtaining. Cotton Batiste fabric in pantaloons and the old fashioned nighties with lots of fullness, suit some of the lighter weight cotton cluneys. Preshrink the cotton type.

CLUNEY

Galloon Lace

This is a term used to describe any lace which has one scalloped edge and one straight edge. A double galloon is one where both edges are scalloped. These are nice for camisole, sleeve, or dress edges.

DOUBLE GALLOON

GUIPURE

Guipure

These are usually produced in tiny edgings suitable for blouse collars, inserts, etc. Most often they are made of cotton in a very heavy look, differentiating between the cluney family of lace. They are more expensive than some laces because of the high density of yarn required to produce the look.

Nylon Lace

Nylon lace is usually a very dainty delicate lace. It tends to be somewhat softer in finish than polyester, although the finish can be regulated by the producer to make it whatever stiffness he desires. It is very durable, washes well and dyes very well. Much of the lingerie lace is nylon.

Polyester Lace

It tends to be a bit heavier than nylon or acetate lace. It is therefore excellent for those beach cover-ups, tablecloths or curtaining. Many of the narrow laces are l00% Polyester, which makes them durable for edgings on children's clothes, blouses, etc. Check the content on your next lace purchase!

Raschel Lace

This is also a type of lace - usually very dainty and patterned for the intimate types of clothing and frilled blouses and dresses. It is often referred to as slip lace. It can come in many fibre qualities from acetate to polyester and nylon.

Stretch Lace

Stretch lace is suitable for body tights, bra sections on nightware in the allover yardage type, but it can give interesting detailing on tricot type lingerie if used in the edging width. Insets under the bra section of a nightie give shaping to the total look. Stretch lace in the very narrow variety is great for waistbands on slips and panty legs. The firmer variety is best here.

LACE REFERENCES *(narrow laces)*

EDGINGS – Any lace having one straight edge which can be applied to finish a garment.

FLAT EYELET

EYELETS – Frilled and flat. These are a cotton with embroidered holes. The embroidery is usually of a silky shiney type giving a dainty appearance. The stitching on European qualities is very fine and intricate, but also more expensive. Frilled eyelets have been pre-gathered, sometimes with a very narrow bias bound top.

BEADING EYELET

BEADING EYELET – This type is used for straps or decorative finishes whereby a ribbon can be inserted. It is finished on both sides so that it can be used as an insertion if so desired.

FAGOTTING – This very interesting trim has been used for centuries. It is very easy to use to dress up an otherwise plain garment. It does give a tailored effect. Generally it is made similar

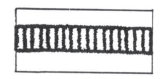

to a guipure type lace (cotton) almost like lattice work, with pieces of fabric running on either side for use as a seam allowance in attaching it to a dress.

FRILLINGS – These are narrow laces of any variety that are pre-gathered with or without a bias bound top. Both the rachel and cluney varieties are available. Generally the guipure laces are not frilled due to the heaviness of the trim. Frillings can vary in width from 3/8″(1m) to 6″ (15.2cm).

LACE APPLICATIONS

Enclosing raw edges on lace applications is always desirable, whether using woven fabric or the traditional tricot type. The following methods can be applied to any fabric.

Finish garment ready for hem to be applied.

Lace extended below fabric

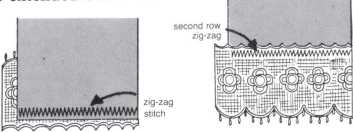

Place lace **wrong side to wrong side** of garment. If "magic tape doesn't mark your fabric you may wish to use it to hold lace in place while you sew. I find that I do not need this as you can easily guide with your hand. Allow lace for upper edge to drop about ⅛"(3mm) below edge of garment. Stitch close to garment edge with tiny zig-zag stitch. Turn down lace. Press lace for upper edge toward garment enclosing raw edge.

Stitch a second row of tiny zig-zag at top of lace through all thicknesses.

Lace applied on top of garment hem

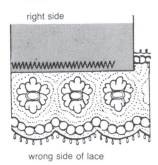
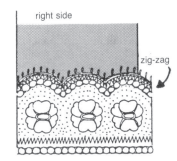

Place only ⅛" (3mm) lace wrong side to wrong side of garment. Stitch on raw edge of garment with a tiny zig-zag. Turn lace up on top of right side of garment hem. Stitch again, following curve of pattern, over bottom and top edges to hold in place.

Lace applied on pre-finished hem edge

If you have a serger you may serge the fabric bottom edge, and then apply lace on top with a tiny zig-zag stitch.

When leaving lace to hang down on a slip edge, make sure it is of a soft quality nylon so that your hosiery will not be ruined.

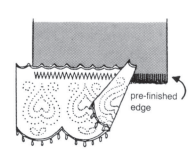

pre-finished edge

Lace Inserts

As lace does not fray it is possible to cut around patterns of your own choosing and apply them to panties, slips, nighties, etc.

The easiest method is to tape the applique on top of the garment with "magic tape" or washable glue stick, and then stitch in place with tiny zig-zag stitches, removing the tape as you stitch. Take your sharp pointed scissors and cut fabric away from behind to within ⅛" (3mm) of stitching. As woven fabrics will not fray on the bias, to leave an unfinished edge should not be a problem. If you do not wish to cut out from behind you may leave the fabric showing through.

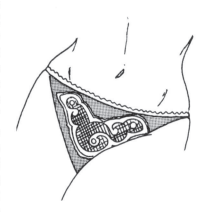

Lace Panels

Apply lace to garment using tiny zig-zag close to edge or carefully following design of lace. It is easiest to cut out garment in full, apply lace inserts and then trim away fabric from behind. If applying with straight of grain on a woven fabric you may want to finish raw edge with serger or tiny zig-zag to eliminate fraying. Plan for this **prior** to applying lace. Place right sides together and stitch when using lace with straight edges if using your serger. This method eliminates use of scolloped edges but is much quicker.

Lace Application for slits on slips

In order to reduce bulk it is advisable to miter the corners. Fold back on mitered line and press with the iron. Cut a ¼″ (6mm) seam allowance. You may overlap these edges and stitch through the middle (trim edges back close to stitching) or stitch in a conventional seam, pressing open.

 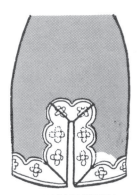

WITH SEAM   WITHOUT SEAM

If using **woven fabrics** you may find it a bit tricky to fold lace back and enclose bottom edges as previously described in Lace Applications. It would be advisable to turn a ⅛″ (3mm) hem to right side of garment and edge stitch. This will then be covered with lace. There are two ways to miter the corners. One is suitable for a side seam, the other for a centre front where there is no seam. Prior to stitching, practice folding lace for mitering, it's easy!

ELASTIC APPLICATIONS

Lingerie coloured elastics are difficult to find in many of the fabric stores. Most of them are made of a rayon type and are not extremely durable. Plush-back elastic is especially nice for lingerie but not always available. It has a soft back which is comfortable next to the skin with a decorative picot edge on the top. It is very attractive for waist edges and panty legs. Polyester types which wear better are usually in white and black only. Chlorine treated elastic is not attractive in appearance but wears extremely well. This is the type of elastic we recommend for **casing** methods.

Transparent elastic one of the newest in the marketplace, lends itself perfectly to the lighter weight silky fabrics. Because of its clear transparency it blends with any colour. It does not pinch or feel tight which makes it perfect for leg and waist areas. At the moment it comes in narrow widths up to ⅝″ (12mm). For more detailed information refer to **Couture Action Knits**, page 97.

Casing Application

This method is best for garments constructed with a straight sewing machine. Sew all seams on garment, side seams, centre front or sleeve seams as applicable.

1. Fold over garment top edge the width of elastic plus seam allowance. Turn under seam allowance just ½″ (1.3cm) and topstitch using small stitch, close to folded edge. leaving a 1″ (25cm) opening near a seam allowance.

2. Cut piece of elastic your waist measurement. Insert elastic (chlorine treated, width desired) through opening and pull ends out. Overlap ends approximately ½" (1.3cm) and stitch together (zig-zag or a multiple stitch).

3. Tuck elastic up in place and stitch across small area left open for elastic insertion.

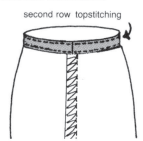

second row topstitching

4. Optional! If desired on **woven fabric,** stitch a row of straight stitching at the very top above elastic. This gives a nice finish on silky fabrics. You may also stitch through all thicknesses on side seam line to keep elastic from moving within casing.

Zig-Zag Application

Ensure that the elastic is durable as this method is very difficult to remove.

If using lingerie elastic take 4 to 6" (10 to l5.3cm) less than waist measurement. Two-thirds of waist measurement is an easy calculation. Sewing several rows of stitching on elastic tends to stretch it out so it is very important to **cut down** on your usual elastic measurement.

1. Overlap elastic ends and stitch back and forth using a zig-zag stitch. A multiple stitch is best.

2. Divide the elastic circle and garment edge in fourths, using pins as markers.

3. Pin elastic to garment outside, having picot edge facing down toward garment, and straight edge at top, matching pin markers.

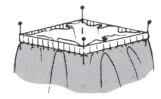

4. Stretch both elastic and garment, stitching the elastic in place, close to picot edge. Use a tiny regular zig-zag or a multiple zig-zag. Should any of the raw edge protrude beyond elastic, trim away.

5. Fold elastic to inside and stitch again, close to straight edge. This will completely enclose the raw edge and give a fabric finish to the right side.

6. In order to give a couture look, take a piece of ribbon or fabric, turning edges in and place over elastic join on inside of waistband. Top stitch in place.

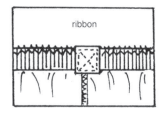

If using a serger, sew garment seams leaving one side seam open. Stitch after applying waist elastic. Cover elastic raw edge joins with a small piece of ribbon stitched as shown in step 6. The entire casing can be stitched with serging. Refer to **Couture Action Knits**, page 100.

> *Top layer of fabric feeding unevenly?* Try lifting presser foot very slightly while sewing. Don't raise the foot...lighten as you sew. Works great!

PANTIES

Commercial panty patterns seem to show raw edge seaming for the crotch area. If using a serger you will usually sew a double crotch directly with panty seam, which is fast but not as finished looking. With silk fabric if the garment is for special evenings, the pattern suggestion for turning under and stitching close to edge for crotch area is adequate. However if you wish to use a cotton or self fabric, enclosed edges are by far the nicest. Here's how you sew them!

1. Sew on any lace motifs while pieces are flat.

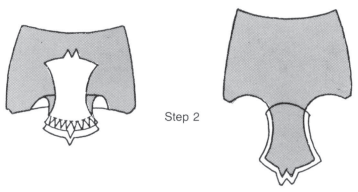

Step 2

2. Take double crotch pieces wrong sides together and sandwich the front crotch panty in between. Use tiny zig-zag or serger if you wish.

3. With right sides together pin back crotch panty to crotch piece as shown.

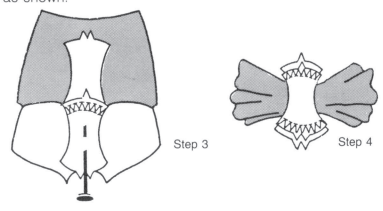

Step 3

Step 4

4. To enclose raw edge, take loose top crotch back around entire panty and key up with other two pinned crotch edges.

5. Trim seams and turn right side out.

6. Using same measurements and methods apply waist and leg elastic as above.

RIBBONS

Polyester Satin ribbon is the easiest ribbon to wash. It is more expensive than acetate ribbons. It does not have as much shine as acetate but the durability is well worth the extra expense. The very narrow ⅛″ (3 cm) works well in beading or thread-through style laces. Join several rows of lace together, interspersing ribbon throughout. This makes a lovely yoke for a nightie. To simplify, cut a piece of brown paper the desired shape. Place rows of lace on paper and steam, shaping as you go.

When completed, pin together and hand or machine stitch. A backing of sheer silk, polyester organza, or sheer tricot will give the lace a foundation when sewn with the garment.

Ribbon Bows

Make or purchase tiny bows for placement at centre front nighties, slips and leg sides.

LACE AND FABRIC DYEING

Most bridal boutiques dye lace and fabrics to match for their specialty designs. This can be rather risky on a commercial level as most fabrics will vary in their ability to dye well. Natural fibres dye best, but the majority of silky synthetics are made with polyester and nylon. Some of the crisper satins are acetate which, being a natural base, would dye easier. Unfortunately the heat required to penetrate the dye into the fabric could take away from the finish.

DYEING METHODS

Hot Method

This is the most desirable method for dyeing in that the permanence is greater. The fabrics best suited to dyeing are Nylon, cotton, linen, wool, silk and viscose Rayon. Reduced shades only are produced with polyesters. Heat water to 60 degrees C, maintain for l5 minutes. It is not advisable to dye acrylics or fabrics with special finishes.

It is possible to dye in your washing machine. However, the home-dye companies do not recommend that wool or silk be dyed in this manner. Use the hottest water setting. Allow the machine to fill with the amount of water for the quantity of cloth you are dyeing. Usually one package of dye will be sufficient for 8 ounces (226 Grams) of dry fabric. Wet the cloth and squeeze out excess moisture. Dissolve dye in two cups of boiling water, adding 1 tbsp. (14 Grams) salt. Add this mixture to machine water and stir. Place fabric in water allowing it to go through longest wash cycle. If you can adjust your cycle, 20 minutes is desirable, followed by a cold rinse. Cotton Batiste (try it on the bias for camisoles and tap pants) is excellent for summer lingerie, and dyes extremely well. It is difficult to find in colours so you may want to try this method, placing the desired white trimming lace in with the fabric. Following this dyeing procedure, **be careful** to run a complete cycle of water through the machine adding one cup of bleach to ensure that no dye is left in the washer.

Polyesters have a very strong texture, making it difficult for dye to penetrate fabric. Try using three tins or packages of dye per 8 ounces (226 GRAMS) of fabric.

Wool and silk can be dyed in a flame proof pan on top of the stove. Use enough water to cover fabric, following same procedure as above, making sure that you keep fabric moving during simmering. Rinse until the water runs clear.

Cold Method

This method will not give the same penetration of colour as the hot method. However, on delicate fabrics or wool, it is the safest. Refer to instructions on dye package.

Lace Dyeing

It is difficult to purchase interesting shades in laces, particularly to match your fabrics. Yarn content will have a great bearing on whether your lace will dye well. Experiment with some inexpensive fabrics, putting your lace in with the dye solution. If laces have blended yarns, a very pleasing two-toned effect can be achieved. Acetate will take the dye extremely well, while polyester (one of the most difficult to dye) will remain almost white. Nylon will sometimes dye a shade darker than your natural type fabrics. Occasionally the contents listed on lace are rather vague and you may come up with a "surprise" after dyeing. Purchase extra as **heat causes shrinkage**. Three inches (7.5cm) per meter would be safe.

DYEING TIPS

★ Put your fabric and trims in the same dye wash. Even if the colour is not exactly the same, it will tone and blend with the garment shade.

★ If using expensive fabrics, always do a sample testing prior to taking the plunge on the entire piece.

★ Dyed garments will hold their colour longer if hand washed with mild soaps and cooler water. However, you can re-dye at a later date if you wish to restore the original shade.

★ With successive dyeing you will master the art and bring colours into your wardrobe that otherwise would not be available.

★ Try mixing dyes to get different tones.

★ Use "tea" to achieve an ecru or ivory shade.

Dyeing can expand your world of colour!

LINGERIE PATTERNS

Every pattern company has a section with lingerie patterns. Some are branching into this area more than before. Several patterns have garments cut on the bias and suggest woven fabrics. Watch for new styles in that section.

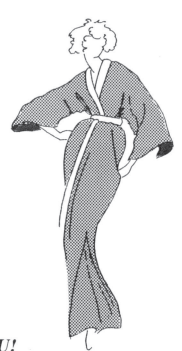

The information on bias in this chapter can help in your pattern adaption. Creating something special for gift-giving could make you a real hit! Robes for men and women are very easy to make. **DON'T FORGET THE MEN IN YOUR LIFE!** Silk robes and shirts are well prized by the men who own them.

PERSONALIZING FOR YOU!

With a little imagination you can become your own designer. If you have favourite pieces of bewitching nightwear, take a similar commercial pattern and modify to your garment specifications. How about that special little boudoir coat to slide over your teddy. Most often they have very straight lines and it would be easy to trace a pattern. Or maybe you don't like the leg shape on the tap pant pattern. Check your favourites and draw a new line. The following is an example of a quick change made from a square leg pattern to a high-leg version. Try it, it's simpler than you think.

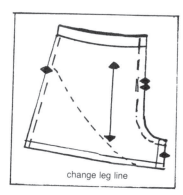

change leg line

NOTES

Let's Make a Teddy

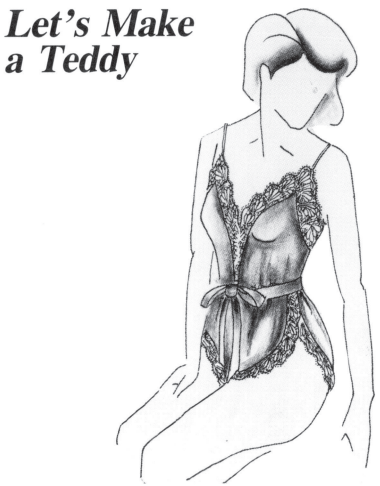

FLIGHT OF FANTASY IN SILK

If you are between a size 8 and 16 this teddy will fit. For those of you that are bigger or smaller it can be graded to some degree. Try it with inexpensive fabric, for your first one. The fit and style are very flattering to the figure. If you are long waisted you may wish to lengthen the bodice or panty pieces, depending on where you need the length. There is nothing more uncomfortable than a teddy that is on the short side. Once you have transferred the pattern onto tracing paper, try it in both a woven fabric on the bias, and a tricot. Add a little "cosmetic" coat and the ensemble is complete.

High-Leg Teddy

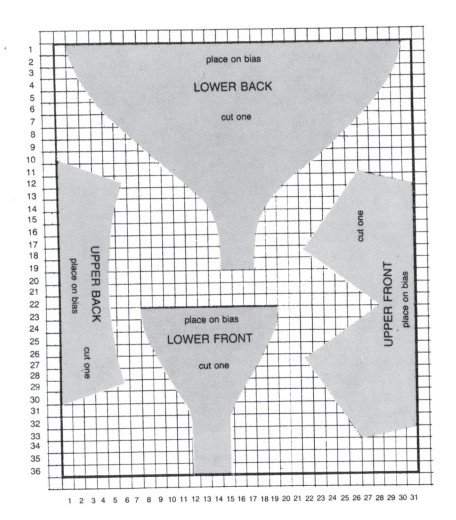

1 SQUARE = 1 INCH (2.54cm)

HIGH-LEG TEDDY

MATERIALS REQUIRED

FABRIC – 1 meter (39.5ins)- 115 cm (45″)width

LACE – 3.5 meters (3⅞ yds) of 5 to 6cm (2 or 2½″ wide edging type flat lace.

ELASTIC – 4 to 6″ (10 to 15cm) less than waist measurement - ¼″ (.5cm) firm lingerie elastic. Chlorine treated is best, if covering with seam allowance, or new transparent type shows fabric colour through.

SUITABLE FABRICS – Polyester or Silk jacquards, crepe de chine, charmeuse, satins, or cotton batiste. Tricot can also be used. No seam finishing necessary with tricot.

SEAMS INCLUDED – Waist Seam- ⅜″ (lcm) or change pattern to ⅝″ (1.5cm) when cutting out, if you wish an enclosed elastic.

Crotch Seam - ⅝″ (1.5cm)
All other Seams- ¼″ (.5cm)
Lace Seams- ¼″ (.5cm)

NOTIONS – 3 clear or coloured snaps. 8″(20.3cm) seam binding to match.

ENGLARGING PATTERN

Using a cardboard cutting board with 2.5cm (1 inch) spaced lines, place see-through tracing cloth (can be purchased in fabric departments) on top of board. Calculate measurements by placing dots on respective lines taken from miniature pattern. Join dots with marking pen (not evaporating type) and cut out pattern. Mark seam allowances on respective areas in order to be sure that you don't forget when sewing teddy. Mark somewhere on your layout for straps, two 1″ (2.5cm) wide bias strips, 20″ (51cm) in length.

CUTTING FABRIC

ALL FABRIC PIECES CUT SINGLE THICKNESS

1. Fold cut edge over to meet selvedge to form bias. Pin to hold edges together.

2. Cut along bias fold line.

3. Slip cutting mat under top piece of bias as shown, leaving bottom piece in place.

4. Place waist edges of lower back and front on fabric as shown. Place weights to hold.

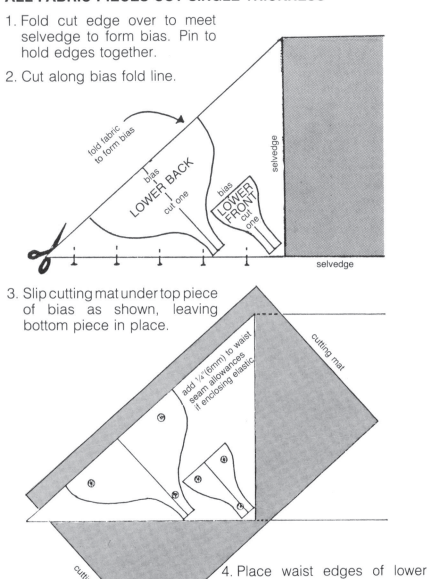

5. Cut with Rotary cutter.

6. Mark center front and back with tiny snips, or marking pen, on waist edges. Transfer other markings.

7. Place cutting board under bottom piece of fabric. Place pattern pieces as shown.

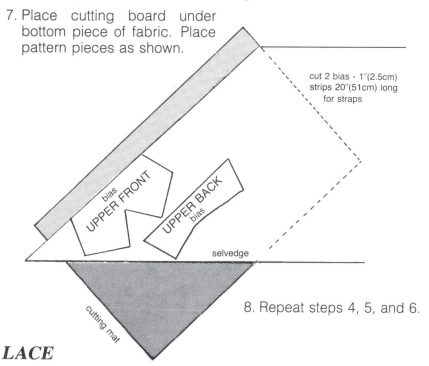

cut 2 bias - 1″(2.5cm) strips 20″(51cm) long for straps

8. Repeat steps 4, 5, and 6.

LACE

SEAM ALLOWANCES – ¼″ (.5 cm)
UPPER BACK – 1 piece 15½″ (39.4cm)
SIDE UPPER FRONTS – 2 pieces 8¾″ (22.3 cm)

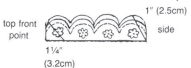

Place the right sides together and trim ends for mitering as shown.

Center Front – Cut 1 piece 19″ (48.3cm) Fold in half right sides together and trim ends for mitering as shown.

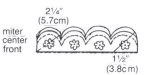

Lower front – Cut 2 pieces 17″ (43cm)

Lower back – Cut 2 pieces 25″ (57cm)

PUTTING IT ALTOGETHER

OPTIONAL – either of two methods may be used for lace application:

A. Conventional right sides together with serged or tiny zig-zag seams.

B. Overlapping lace and stitching in centre or finishing raw edge of fabric first and then applying lace on top, stitching with tiny zig-zag stitch.

Both methods are used with the teddy. The top has the lace applied on top which allows the tiny bottom scalloped edge of lace to show and the panty section has the conventional ¼" seam. You may choose to alter these methods.

Staystitch

As Teddy is cut on bias, it is necessary to stabilize edges. Staystitch leg edges, front and back, ¼" (.5cm) in from edges. Repeat step on upper front and back pieces. If serging top edges on bodice, staystitch following that step.

1. **LOWER BACK** – On both sides of back, pin right sides together, lace and fabric. Begin tapering lace approximately 3½"(9cm) up from lower edge, to ⅝" (1.5cm) showing on sides at crotch.

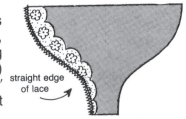

straight edge of lace

Pull stay-stitch to make garment fit the lace. Put most of fullness over seat area. Garment will cup slightly giving back shape. Press over ham, shrinking fullness.

2. Use serger and stitch ¼" (.5cm) seam. Tiny zig-zag or small overcast type seam is also suitable.

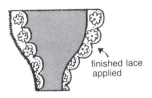

finished lace applied

3. **LOWER FRONT** – Same as Lower Back, Step 1 and 2.

4. Place front on top of back matching up large circles. Baste stitch lace overlap.

5. **UPPER BACK** – Serge ¼″ (.5cm) seam (other suggested stitches can be used), on upper edge. Overlap straight edge of lace, the

width of serging, wrong side to right side of back, and using tiny zig-zag, top-stitch close to edge of lace, easing as necessary.

6. **UPPER FRONT** – Serge top edges. Baste mitered points of lace, upper fronts together to determine if adjustment is necessary. Pull stay-stitching on bodice to fit lace. Lace will cup at top points giving good fit over bust area. If you are smaller, you may release the basting on miters and flatten.

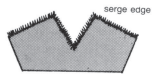

serge edge

7. a) Serge center front lace, as fitted. b) Join centre front to side front lace, right sides together at top point. (could overlap and stitch if you prefer).

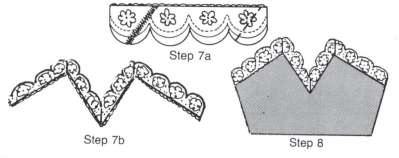

Step 7a

Step 7b

Step 8

8. Pin lace on upper front edges. Stitch in place as in Step 5 upper back.

9. Serge stitch side seams together on upper bodice.

10. Place bottom inside top right sides together, matching center fronts to backs, and large square to side seam. Baste stitch together in ⅜″ (1cm) seam or ⅝″ (1.5cm) if allowing for enclosed elastic. Try on; tie ribbon around waist. Adjust waist seam until front lays flat for your figure.

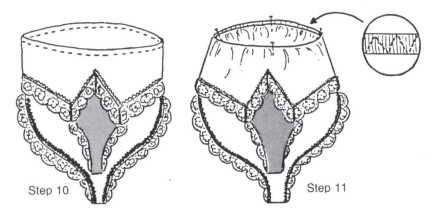

Step 10   Step 11

11. **ELASTIC** – Take a piece of elastic 4 to 6″(10 to 15cm) less than your waist measurement depending on the amount of stretch. If enclosing, you may use chlorine treated elastic as it will wear much better than others. If exposed, you may want to colour co-ordinate with garment, or use transparent elastic. Refer to page 102, Zig-zag Elastic Application for details on applying to waist seam. Step 3 will be modified - Pin elastic to garment **inside**. Use a multiple zig-zag if you have it or you can serge the elastic in place. Stop at Step 4.

12. Turn garment to right side. Pushing seam allowances toward bodice, top-stitch from the right side, catching top edge of elastic, using tiny zig-zag stitch.

13. **STRAPS** – Refer to Bias Tubing, page for instructions on making straps. You may also use regular ribbon and extenders if able to purchase the colour needed for garment. At this point try on teddy again, pinning crotch and straps in place to determine proper length.

PLACEMENT OF STRAPS:

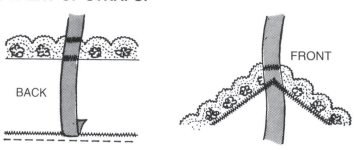

BACK – Lay on waist seam, edges together, strap facing toward bottom of garment. Zig-zag stitch close to edge, then flip up toward top back edge. Use tiny zig-zag stitch at top and bottom edge of lace.

FRONT – attach as shown, zig-zag at top and bottom edges of lace, leaving extension of strap into bodice or tucking it under prior to zig-zagging.

14. **CROTCH** – Turn under ⅝″ (1.5cm) seam on front crotch. Turn back crotch over ⅝″ (1.5cm) to right side. If hidden snaps are desired, see below. Place matching coloured seam binding over seam allowance and topstitch top and bottom  edges. Sew three clear snaps on tape. Metal snaps can be sewn to seam allowance before binding is applied. Place seam binding over snaps and topstitch in place, using zipper foot. Hand tack seam binding to snaps. Make pin pricks for snaps to poke through. Use fray check as necessary. If fine type snap tape is available you may purchase it in a co-ordinating colour. The heavy twill tape with the snaps far apart is not suitable.

Fourteen steps to put you on a "Flight of Fantasy"

Special Treatments

APPLIQUE ARTISTRY

Unique personalized treatments can be achieved by the use of applique. Cutting out a flower or leaf from a designer fabric and placing it strategically on your garment will add interest to an otherwise plain style. Machine applique is by far the quickest method, but hand applique is also acceptable. Always try a sample on a scrap of fabric to decide on its suitability.

Machine Applique

IRON-ON FUSING APPLIED

1. Place a small piece of light weight iron-on fusing behind flower or leaf. Using sharp small scissors or rotary wheel, cut out design. This step gives stability in cutting of intricate patterns and eliminates fraying.

2. Choose a fine thread with some sheen if possible. Cotton or blend type thread tends to dry out over a period of time. Placing **thread in fridge** for several hours will put moisture back into humidity chambers, and increases vibrancy of colour. Thread will also be smoother giving embroidery a neater finish.

3. You may want to use "Transfuse"™ which will put a fusible back to your applique. This then makes it very easy to fuse the applique in place, prior to stitching. You may also use fusible web but this is difficult to cut out and place properly, on it's own. Once purchased, this reusable transfuse sheet will last for years. It is also possible to place "tear away" non-woven cloth (available in fabric stores) on wrong side of garment which gives stability to applique while sewing. This piece is ripped or removed from back at conclusion of machine stitching. If you wish to "pad" the applique you **should not fuse** the applique to the garment but use magic transparent tape for placement. Using embroidery hoop, centre design in circle.

EMBROIDERY HOOP

4. With embroidery hoop in place, slip garment under presser foot. Set your stitch at 1.5 or 2.0mm width zig-zag and .45 or .50 in length. Loosen the upper tension to approximately 3. Some of the newer machines have a slightly slanted zig-zag which seems to produce excellent embroidery. Zig-zag close to edge of applique enclosing raw edges, removing tape as you come to it. If desired, a row of straight stitching around pattern strikes a finishing accent. Some machines have embroidery feet making it easier to see your work as you stitch.

PADDED APPLIQUE –Refer to Step 3. Remove backing "stitch and tear" type if used. Carefully slit small opening in back of applique with tiny scissors. Place desired amount of poly fibre-fill inside. Sew up slit, using tiny hand stitches. If necessary, you may use liquid Fray-check to eliminate fraying.

INITIALS

Applique initials can be stitched on your machine if you have mastered the embroidery stitches. A sample initial would be a must to determine if your fabric will lend itself to that amount of stitching or whether puckering will take place. The easiest types, are the new sew-on or iron-on initials which are available in your notions departments. This addition to a shirt top can give a couturier look, with very little effort.

FABRIC BUTTONS (CHINESE BALL)

Using self-filled or corded tubing, see page 91, with pieces approximately 16″ (40.6cm) twist as per following diagrams. Be sure to keep seam facing you as you twist. When totally twisted - draw the ends, pulling the loops tightly together to form a little ball.

FROG CLOSURE

Some shaping may be required with your fingers. Clip off excess and secure ends to back of button with tiny hand stitches. This button uses either a thread or bias tubing buttonloop or a frog closure.

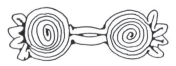

Here is another variation of the frog closure, achieved using bias tubing. Simply form a tight circle with decorative picot edge.

Tack from behind to secure. Extend bias across pre-stitched buttonhole slit and form a second circle. Secure as above.

ROSETTES

Using a very short length of narrow bias tubing, (usually same fabric as garment) twist in small cirle forming the centre of rosette. Use tiny hand stitches to hold in place. Gather along a straight lace edging, usually ⅝" (1.5cm) pulling up tightly. Place underneath bias centre. and tack together. If desired a contrast coloured french knot can be worked on the top centre. These give a nice finishing touch to the centre front of a nightie or use a larger version on matching slippers.

FEATHERS

Feathers add a soft edging to evening and loungewear. Maribou feathers as they are called, are purchased by the hank, which is usually 2 1/2 feet (76.2cm) in length. These are applied to a garment in the following method to allow for easy removal for washing or drycleaning your garment. Make 1/2 inch (1.3cm) thread loops approximately every 4 inches around the garment. Thread feathers carefully through these loops, attaching at each end. Fluff feathers around loops.

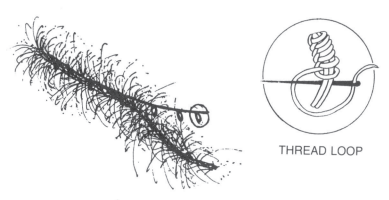

THREAD LOOP

PIN TUCKING

This treatment is interesting on silk fabric. It gives a special look without detracting from the beauty of the fabric and is relatively easy to produce. Try it on a bodice or blouse front, pocket or yoke. Pin tucking prior to cutting out garment is by far the easiest. A normal series of up to six pin tucks is made with a space in between the next group. Use a fine twin needle. Measure and mark lines for pintucking with scissor snips or marking pen on seam allowances. Fold back approximate line for first row and press with iron. Centre machine needles over fold line using small stitches. Continue stitching successive rows using edge guide if necessary.

Thread loops are much easier to make with embroidery cotton.

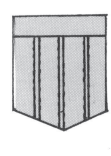

Most sewing machine books give detailed instruction for their machine. Some of the newer machines have a special Cording Tongue which hooks onto the throat plate whereby a buttonhole twist thread or crochet cotton (preshrunk) is incorporated into the underside of the stitching, creating a corded effect. A special clear foot with grooves on the underside is also used with this technique. Wider tucks are also very attractive and relatively simple to stitch. Refer to your basic sewing book if you need further instruction.

Pintucking can also be done with the serger by using the rolled edge finish. Refer to **COUTURE ACTION KNITS** book, page 122 for ideas on mock French hand sewing done by machine.

SLIPPERS

There is always enough to make a matching pair of "silk slippers" with the scraps from your bias cut lingerie. Use one of the rosettes to decorate the top and some pressed type fleece for the filler on the sole. Your gift giving opportunities will increase! Use a commercial pattern if you are unsure of methods.

LEFTOVER SCRAPS

The luscious hand of silk will encourage you to take care in cutting garments, to enable you the best advantage for workable leftovers. Beautiful silk scarves, belts, jewellery bags, little pillows, sachets and a "silk garter" for that special bride, can all be made from scraps.

INDEX

AVAILABLE FROM TEX-MAR SEMINARS AND PUBLICATIONS

PUBLICATIONS

1. **"COUTURE ACTION KNITS", THE GUIDEBOOK TO SEWING WITH 'KNIT KNOW HOW'** , including Overlock Serging techniques, by **HAZEL BOYD HOOEY**

2. **"SILKS & SATINS" – TWENTY-FOUR HOUR ELEGANCE, THE SEWING GUIDEBOOK TO FASHIONS IN SILK,** by **HAZEL BOYD HOOEY**

SEMINARS (Lecture, Slide and Fashion Show presentations)

1. **"COUTURE ACTION KNITS"**

2. **"SILKS & SATINS" – TWENTY-FOUR HOUR ELEGANCE**

For information on hosting a Tex-Mar seminar, to order publications, **OR TO PASS ON A COMMENT** contact:

TEX-MAR SEMINARS AND PUBLICATIONS
#57 — 10220 DUNOON DRIVE
RICHMOND, BRITISH COLUMBIA
V7A 1V6
(604-277-3231)